THE STORM PETREL
AND THE
OWL OF ATHENA

Everything, like the ocean,
Flows and comes into contact
with everything else:
touch it in one place
and it reverberates
at the other end of the world.

DOSTOYEVSKY

THE STORM PETREL
AND THE
OWL OF ATHENA

BY LOUIS J. HALLE

PRINCETON UNIVERSITY PRESS, 1970

PRINCETON, NEW JERSEY

THIS volume, as the reader will see, contains two books that make up one. Parts One and Two, although superficially different, tend to repeat each other in their underlying thought like a theme and variations in music. The way they do so became fully clear to me only when I was completing the preparation of the whole for publication. This requires explanation.

Every book is the product of a partnership between author and publisher, but in the case of this book the collaboration has been of a special kind. I exemplify this by noting that the selection and arrangement of the contents in Part Two has been entirely the work of Herbert S. Bailey, Jr., Director of the Princeton University Press. What I did was merely to send him the short pieces on nature, or topics closely related to nature, that I had written over the years. The selections he made from this accumulation, and the order in which he proposed that they appear, are represented exactly by Part Two as it now stands. I had no change to suggest. The reader will see how, underlying a diversity of material, some of it light-hearted in its expression, one theme and one philosophical vision develops cumulatively in Parts One and Two alike, culminating respectively in two Epilogues that, utterly different as they are, represent the same conclusion. I was myself surprised and pleased to see the way in which, for the most part, each section of Part Two tended to lead implicitly into what followed. I don't know who other than Mr. Bailey would have had the kind of sensitive understanding and intelligence this represents. His selection and arrangement was a creative act for which I am grateful.

I have followed the widespread practice, at least in the scientific literature, of capitalizing the vernacular names of species, but only when given in their entirety: e.g., "Among the hundreds of Arctic Terns one tern alone was in the immature plumage."

By providing a bibliography I have dispensed with the need for complete identification in the text of the sources cited.

ACKNOWLEDGMENTS

Messrs. T. M. Y. Manson of Lerwick, Oliver Ashford, and Paul Géroudet (both of Geneva) read the text of Part One critically, and I have each to thank for amplifications or corrections. Mr. E. Binder of Geneva's Muséum d'Histoire naturelle kindly supplied me with information that enabled me to be accurate on a scientific point. An ornithologist who must here be nameless rendered an invaluable service in forcing me, by his questioning, to make explicit in an Epilogue to Part One the philosophical doubt and heterodoxy that were only implicit in its Chapter VIII.

Messrs. Bailey and P. J. Conkwright together designed the physical arrangement and format of this volume with exceptional conscience and taste. Their task was not eased by having to make the best of illustrations that, especially in their technical aspects, betrayed my own lack of training in the graphic arts. The justification for using them at all, rather than commissioning the work of a professional, was that they and the text they illustrate, coming from the same hand, were bound to represent the vision of the same eye.

I am most grateful to Miss Ulrike Wuttig for much typing and checking, and for serving what I should like to believe is the purpose of existence itself by bringing order out of chaos. I have her to thank, as well, for the authorship of the Index.

I am indebted to Robin Halle for letting me use photographs by him as a basis for several drawings in Part One, and to M. Paul Géroudet for permission to use a photograph taken by him of an Arctic Tern as the basis for the drawings on pages 55 and 66.

In Part One, the epigraph of Chapter II is from Kipling's "The Last Chantey." The epigraphs of Chapter III, of the section of Chapter VII beginning on page 99, and of Chapter VIII are from "The Birds" by J. C. Squire, printed here with the kind permission of Mr. Raglan Squire and Macmillan & Company, Ltd., publishers of his *Collected Poems*, London, 1959. The epigraph of the Epilogue is taken from *Einstein: His Life and Times* by Philipp Frank (Alfred A. Knopf, New York, 1965, p. 284) with the kind permission of the publisher.

Referring to Part Two: "The Water Rail" was privately printed for *The New Republic* in 1963 by the firm of E. J. Brill in Leiden, Holland, and parts of it appeared respectively in the *Atlantic Naturalist* of July-September 1958 and in *The New Republic* of March 23, 1959 (I here renew my original dedication of it to Gilbert A. Harrison, Editor-in-Chief of *The New Republic*); "The Marsh Terns," "Alpine Choughs in a Valley," "The Concept of Species," and "The Refugee Species" first appeared respectively in the issues of *Atlantic Naturalist* for October-December 1967, January-March 1959, July-September 1961, and April-June 1963; "Scene: Geneva . . ." appeared in *The New Republic* of June 19, 1961; "The Parish of America" first appeared in *The Bulletin of the Massachusetts Audubon Society* of January 1948; "Hudson's Pampas Today" first appeared in *Audubon Magazine*, issue of July-August 1948; "On Rereading 'Green Mansions' " first appeared in the issue of *The Land* for Winter 1947-1948, and then in *Forever the Land*, an anthology edited by Russell and Kate Lord, published by Harper & Brothers in 1950 (to my surprise it was also used by the original American publisher of *Green Mansions* in 1959 as an introduction to a spectacular edition containing illustrations that, when the edition had first appeared in 1943, had been the occasion of my critical comment in the opening paragraph); "The Owl of Athena" first appeared in *University*, issue of Summer-Fall 1963; and "The Religion of Sedge" first appeared in my *Sedge*, published by Frederick A. Praeger, Inc., New York, in 1963. I am grateful to the magazines and publishers named above for permission to use these pieces here.

L. J. H.

Geneva, 1969

CONTENTS

North + Pole

Franz Josef Land

Spitzbergen

GREENLAND

ICELAND

ARCTIC CIRCLE

Faroe

Shetland

Hebrides   Orkney

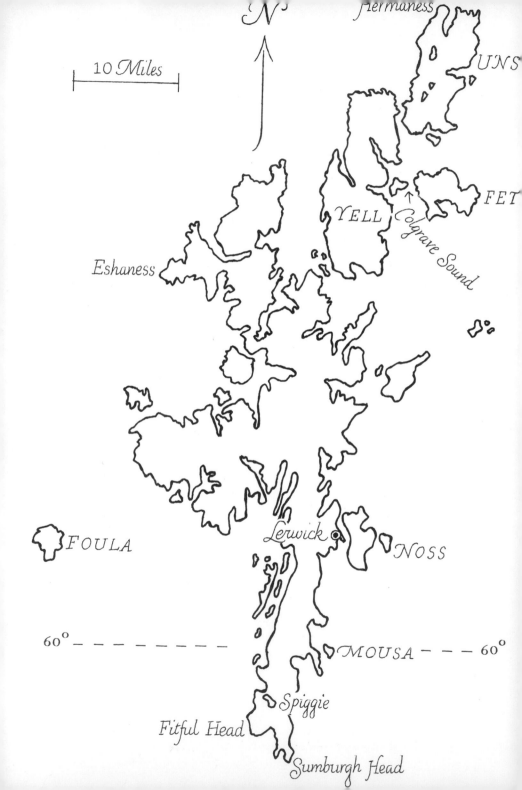

PART ONE

FROM ANOTHER WORLD

Cliffs of Foula

INTRODUCTION

THE birth of an interest in birds usually comes in late childhood and as a result of association with grownups who go in for the observation of local species. By contrast, my own interest was born when, already an undergraduate, I read in William Beebe's *Arcturus Adventure* an account of the Wandering Albatross. Having to know more about it immediately, I explored what other books had to offer, and so came upon W. B. Alexander's *Birds of the Ocean*, which aroused my interest in seabirds generally. During those first weeks my observations were all pursued through the pages of books, and they were of birds that, so far from occurring locally, belonged to another world from the one I inhabited. I pursued them with such zeal, however, that I soon was well informed on the taxonomy, the habitats, the ranges, the migrations, and the behavior of the world's seabirds, especially of the most distant ones, those found in the circumpolar ocean of the southern hemisphere. I became remarkably familiar with birds I had never seen and had no prospect of seeing.

My pursuit of birds did not long remain confined to books. During the summers at my home outside New York, in default of albatrosses I gave myself body and soul to the observation of the local birds. There is a kind of obsessive passion that is lost as youth gives way to middle age. For a number of years after the albatross first put me under a spell I lived half my imaginative life in the world of birds, wherever I was physically or whatever I was outwardly occupied in doing. At one time I knew nothing in the world as well as the contents of Chapman's *Handbook of Birds of Eastern North America*. There is bound to be some embarrassment in recalling such an obsession forty years later, just as it is embarrassing to recall a seizure of "puppy" love when one was fifteen, although the purity and intensity of such a love can never again be equaled. Those of us who have long outgrown these experiences must view them with indulgence.

Through all the years when I was pursuing my love—tracking local birds over field and meadow, through woods and swamps—the seabirds remained in my imagination as the paragons of nature. They also remained, for the most part, beyond my physical horizons. On an occasional sea voyage from the east coast of the United States to the Gulf of Honduras I sometimes saw an isolated skua, shearwater, or tropic-bird. Along the Caribbean shores where I sometimes wandered I became familiar with pelicans, boobies, and those aerial prodigies, the frigate birds; but these were all coastal birds. They were not truly pelagic birds, such as occur in their great concentrations only in the high latitudes of the northern or southern hemisphere. From the coast of Massachusetts, looking seaward, I once saw two black specks that were either murres or Razor-billed Auks; and once from the south shore of Long Island I saw what I was almost sure were Kittiwakes (if only they had been not quite so far away!). That was about all the direct experience of seabirds I had.

Meanwhile I grew older and there was less time for birds. ("Less time" is what one says, but what one means is that the passion of youth has been spent.) Circumstances brought me to live in Europe, on the shores of the Lake of Geneva, where I continued my pursuit of birds, albeit less intensely. Life was too crowded. There was no time (let us say) to master the birds of Europe as I had once mastered those of eastern North America. And one instinctively hesitated, after passing the half-century mark, to subject oneself to circumstances in which there was no blinking the fact that one's eyes and ears were losing their keenness.

What I am leading up to is the experience of suddenly finding myself in Shetland, that little archipelago which stands remote in seas far to the north of mainland Scotland, and finding myself there at the time of year when the great seabird populations, gathered together from all over the ocean, had assembled in their thousands and their tens of thousands for the nesting season. It was a miracle. After all these years, when I no longer looked for it, the portals had opened before me. Here, at last, were the birds I had lived with, in imagination only, over so many years. At once the old passion was rekindled.

During sixteen days in Shetland, at a time of year when birding could be pursued all night as well as all day, there were bound to be observations that seemed worth noting, and so I made notes. Back in Switzerland I was moved to set down some of these observations, while they were still fresh, in two or three articles for periodical publication. The undertaking, however, as I proceeded with it, developed its own momentum, its own seriousness, and even its own theme. The result is the chapters that follow.

In these chapters I have concentrated on the seabirds, partly because they are the most conspicuous and numerous of the Shetland birds, partly because, as representatives of a world outside the one that is familiar to us, they enlarge our perspective of nature, but chiefly because they are my first love, to which I have remained faithful (in my fashion). There was no reason, however, why I should confine myself entirely to them, and in any case they do not constitute a clear category.

My subject is ostensibly the birds of Shetland—but there is no species of bird that belongs just to Shetland. British bird-watchers are accustomed to thinking of all the birds in Britain as "British birds," a conception that can distort one's perspective. To take one example: the account of the Great Skua in *The Handbook of*

British Birds would lead anyone to believe it was a "British bird" with colonial outposts in the antarctic, rather than, what it is, an abundant bird of the antarctic that has, remarkably enough, established a remote outpost in the northeastern corner of the Atlantic. In point of fact, there is not a single species of bird that even approaches being exclusive to the British Isles, let alone to Shetland.

The concept of "British birds" represents a traditional way of thinking that goes back at least to the days of Gilbert White, when few Englishmen had occasion to live in a world larger than their homeland. White and his contemporaries were in no position to appreciate such species as they observed locally in terms of the global setting, as items in the avifauna of what is one world; and old habits of thought persist even now, when it has at last become unthinkable to seek a rounded understanding of any species without viewing it in terms of its entire geographical range.

The fault is not confined to the British. I doubt that many of my fellow countrymen ever think of the species of mockingbird that occurs in the United States as merely the local representative of a series of species that extends to southern South America—or ever think of the big red-breasted thrush that we call the American Robin as only one of a series of such thrushes that occur throughout the hemisphere. And there is a general impression among them that the Everglade Kite, which is common on the Argentine pampas, is on the verge of extinction, simply because its population in the United States (a colony on the tip of Florida, at the extreme northern end of its range) is close to the point of disappearance.

Since my own interest in birds began with the Wandering Albatross, rather than with any bird that occurred within five thousand miles of where I lived, my own disposition has been to see birds in global terms. My observations in Shetland, then, are not of

Shetland birds. They are of birds that belong to the wide world, although it was in Shetland that I saw them.

The parochialism we have all inherited, although now obsolete, accounts for a vernacular nomenclature that creates a problem for anyone who is writing about birds in global terms. The British refer to "the Cormorant," "the Curlew," "the Swift," "the Kingfisher," "the Wren," etc., not providing adjectives to distinguish them from others of their kind because the others do not normally occur in the British Isles, however common they may be across the Channel or across the Atlantic. This deficiency is just beginning to be corrected now that we have a field guide in English that covers Britain and the continent together. Happily, Messrs. Peterson, Mountfort, and Hollom, in the latest edition of their *Field Guide to the Birds of Britain and Europe*, have renamed "the Heron" "the Gray Heron," "the Kite" "the Red Kite," thereby providing relief for us continental bird-watchers when we have to distinguish, in English, among different species of heron or kite.

A more intractable problem is that of different British and American names for the same species. What the British call the "Gray Phalarope" we Americans call the "Red Phalarope"; what they call the "Red-necked Phalarope" we call the "Northern Phalarope." Worse yet, a circumpolar species is called the "Common Gull" in Britain (where it is far from being as common as other species), the "Short-billed Gull" in America, and the "Mew Gull" elsewhere. If one is writing for a combined audience, British and American, what is one to do? British readers may not recognize the "Parasitic Jaeger" as being their "Arctic Skua," Americans may not recognize the "Arctic Skua" as being their "Parasitic Jaeger."

Rather than following one consistent principle in dealing with this dilemma, I have, in each instance, followed my own taste. "Loon," to my taste, is a better term than "diver." I also prefer "murre" for the genus *Uria*, reserving "guillemot" for *Cepphus*. On the other hand, being more of a "lumper" than a "splitter" when it comes to classification of any kind, I prefer to apply the generic name "skua" to all the species of the genus *Stercorarius*, rather than apply it to one only, calling the other three "jaegers." In the many cases where I have no decided preference I have used the British term simply because my observations were of the species on the British side of the Atlantic, where no other usage in speech would be normal. However, to enable the reader to work his own way out of the inevitable confusion, I have presented, in connection with the Index, an alphabetical list of all the birds mentioned in the text (of Part II as well as Part I), first giving the vernacular name, then the scientific name, then any alternative vernacular name, whether British or American.

With the world continuing to shrink, however, let me here make a plea for the standardization and rationalization of the English vernacular nomenclature of species that are, after all, cosmopolitan. This could be achieved either by agreement among the official ornithological organizations of the respective countries (through the agency of a joint committee on vernacular nomenclature), or less officially by the authors of standard field guides, who have already made a good start in this direction (e.g., the introduction of the term "Peregrine Falcon" alongside "Duck Hawk" in Peterson's American field guides, and the addition of adjectives that I have already mentioned in the equivalent field guide for "Britain and Europe").

Finally, there is an isolated anomaly of vernacular nomenclature that is without justification. All the species of the family *Hydrobatidae* are known, in their collectivity, as the "storm petrels," and one of those species in particular, *Hydrobates pelagicus*, is also known as the "Storm Petrel." This poses the problem of avoiding such absurdities as: "The sea was covered with storm petrels, among which a number of Storm Petrels could be distinguished." Let the matter be corrected!

DEDICATION

My wife conspired with Oliver and Lilias Ashford to get me to Shetland. This was a delicate matter, since I was bound to say I had too much to do. So the three of them gave me no more than an occasional hint of what they were up to. Being a man of decision, I responded on each occasion by making it crystal clear that I could not commit myself. By late June, however, it transpired that two cottages had been rented and travel reservations made. Although I never said I would go, I went.

In addition to the two aforementioned Ashfords and my wife, I found a second generation of Halles—Julia, Mark, Robin, and Anne—going along as well. In Shetland we were joined by a second generation of Ashfords, Richard and (by marriage) Kay, who came up from Nigeria accompanied by a third generation in the person of George Oliver Ashford, then five months old. Later, Richard and Elizabeth Ashford Winter (second generation) joined us, coming from London.

To GEORGE OLIVER ASHFORD (whose name is magnified for the occasion) I most especially dedicate these observations, if only because he has the longest life-expectancy of any of us.

I have rarely been so grateful to anyone as I am to the three conspirators, and my heart goes out with appreciation to all who finally made up our band of Shetland invaders. If these observations are most especially dedicated to George Oliver Ashford, they are only less especially dedicated to all the others.

L. J. H.

It is no use speaking of the great

ocean to the frog in the well. —CHUANG-TZU

I. FROM ANOTHER WORLD

THE birds whose lives are the most remote from human knowledge are those that spend them far from land in the wastes of the ocean. Even when they come to land for breeding, as they must, it may be only at night, and then only to disappear into underground burrows or fissures of rock.

Most of us know such birds, if at all, by seeing them from shipboard. If they are large birds that follow ships, we then have an opportunity to familiarize ourselves with them in these limited circumstances. But the birds I am about to treat of here, although they do follow ships, are the smallest of seabirds. All one sees, ordinarily, is fluttering specks in the trough of the wave.

The order *Procellariiformes* combines an exceptional distinctiveness with a variety exemplified by the fact that it includes both the largest and the smallest of all the seabirds that fly: the Wandering Albatross, with a wingspread of almost twelve feet, and the Storm Petrel, the size of a swallow. In between are a wide assortment of petrels and shearwaters.

On the wing or on the wave the Storm Petrel, only six inches long, appears all black except for a flashing white rump. At sea it dangles its delicate feet to patter over the waves in fluttering flight. When oceanic storms rage for days, with the great combers incessantly crashing along their courses, this little bird somehow survives. Either it must be constantly fluttering in the turbulence without sleep, or it is able to sleep head-under-wing on the tumultuous surface, tossed to the

sky, caught in the shattering whitecap, dropped again
into the depth of the trough. There is reason to doubt
that it makes much distinction between night and day
at sea, although it is strictly nocturnal on its breeding
grounds.

One of the breeding places is the uninhabited island
of Mousa in Shetland. Mousa is less than a mile and a
half in its greatest length, hardly more than a thousand
yards in its greatest width. A rockbound coast encloses
the usual moors of grass, heather, and sphagnum moss,
on which sheep and Shetland ponies graze, on which
Great Skuas and Arctic Skuas breed; also the usual
peat bogs, and a fresh-water loch on which Red-throated
Loons raise their young.

This island has, however, a distinction and a fame
that have nothing to do with birds. On it is the best
preserved of those prehistoric fortresses called "brochs,"
of which some five hundred are still identifiable in
remains scattered over the mainland and the islands
of northern Scotland. The birds that are the subject of
this chapter, and about which so little can be known,
are associated (as we shall see) with the Broch of
Mousa, about which virtually nothing is known.

It is a round tower on the coast, forty-three feet
high and fifty feet in diameter at its base. It slopes
inward in a curve that is convex in its lower half, and
slightly concave in its upper, to a summit forty feet in
diameter. The construction is of uncut local stones that
are, for the most part, naturally flat and no larger than
what one could pick up with one hand—a primitive
construction lacking cement. Nevertheless, it is tight,
its solidity attested by the fact that the broch has
endured the high winds of Shetland since the time of
Christ. Its wall is some fifteen feet thick at the base,
but on the inside it accommodates in its thickness
chambers or galleries, as well as a staircase that winds
to the summit. (As we shall see, it accommodates more
than that in its thickness.) The outside is uniform and

unbroken except for one small entrance. Those who took refuge inside could cut themselves off from the world, withstanding its assault.

The Shetlanders incline to believe that the brochs were built by the Picts, but we know virtually nothing about these people whom the Romans encountered over three hundred miles farther south, in Scotland proper, and we have no knowledge that they were ever in these islands.

The same local stones as were used so long ago to build the Broch of Mousa were used in recent times for shoulder-high stone walls in the vicinity of the broch, and for a crofter's house that is falling into ruin now that the island is no longer inhabited. Although these are modern structures, they are of the same construction as the broch.

Visiting the broch in broad daylight one would have no way of knowing that there was life inside the thickness of its wall, or inside the surrounding stone fences. Only by taking the wall apart could one find any evidence of it, but what one then found would be astonishing.

Although Storm Petrels are strictly nocturnal on their nesting grounds, there is no real night in Shetland in July. Instead of darkness there is a dusk that merges into dawn. The sun sets in the northwest about ten o'clock, but the sunset glow remains, moving along the northern horizon until, about four in the morning, now in the northeast, it becomes the sunrise. At the darkest hour, about one, some stars are visible and one can see (as we did on Mousa) a satellite passing north-to-south across the sky. But one could read a book by the light that remains, and the activity of birds is never stilled. All night the gulls and skuas, reduced to silhouettes against the sky, pass overhead crying. All night the Fulmars sweep along the shores or, crossing the island, rise and dip over the contours of its hills.

We had arranged for a boatman to take us to the island at ten in the evening of July 13, 1968, and to come for us again at eight the next morning. The sky was clear of clouds all night and the next day. We walked across the moors from our landing-place, and it was eleven o'clock, with the dusk thickening, when we came to the first of the high stone walls in the vicinity of the broch. Here a low sound pervaded the atmosphere, a continuous and invariable sound that one would say was produced by some small clockwork device with whirring wheels. It was intermediate between the purring of a cat and the softest snoring, all on one pitch but interrupted with perfect regularity, every two or three seconds, by an indescribable single note. One had the impression that it came from a distance until, trying to locate it, one found that, in fact, its source was inside the stone wall only inches away. I could not believe that a bird was inside, producing such a sound. Perhaps an insect, or a small frog.

Mated Storm Petrels relieve each other at the nest every two or, sometimes, three days, the relieved bird spending its leave at sea while the other sits in confinement. We were told that, because they are reluctant to come to land except under cover of true darkness, on cloudless nights at this latitude there are fewer exchanges than usual at the nests. Even well after midnight there was still no sign of such activity. At 12:20, however, standing by a broken-down part of a stone wall from which the buzzing came, we had the impression of a small bird darting into it. A moment later we thought we saw one darting out again (it might have been a Wheatear), and the sound had stopped.

At 12:53, standing by the broch, suddenly we found ourselves surrounded by darting and fluttering shapes. All around the tower, at this darkest hour of the night, was a swarm of what might have been bats—but perfectly silent, with not even a sound from their wings when they almost grazed us. It was hard to make out the features of any individual, since one's eye could hardly follow, in such deep twilight and so near at hand, the swift erratic course of a single bird. They moved for the most part close to the wall, up or down as much as horizontally.

With thousands of undifferentiated chinks between stones, it would be a wonder if any bird could find the one that led to its own nest. Here the utility of the continuous snoring signal became apparent. Some birds seemed to find the right opening at once, whereupon they would quickly squeeze themselves through it, disappearing into the wall. Others were obviously having a hard time. They would flutter vertically up and down the wall, trying to insert themselves into openings that were too small. Sometimes one would, in its flight, swing like a pendulum back and forth along the wall.

One was trying endlessly to find a way into the wall at a place, about three feet above the ground, from which the snoring came. It would cling vertically to the

wall with its feet, its wings open and fluttering from moment to moment, its tail spread and the white rump conspicuous, trying to force its head into little openings. One of our party put his hand over it and plucked it from the wall. It was gentle in the hand as we felt the soft depths of its feathered blackness, as we examined the black wires of its feet and the delicately polished black bill—the compound bill, in miniature, of all its order, of the great albatross itself, with an open tube on top. Its jet eye, looking upon us, seemed gentle and indifferent. Released, it darted away, but soon was back, engaged in what seemed a frantic and fruitless search of an area two or three feet square; while, from inside, the mechanical whirring went on without variation. The bird would go away and return to resume the search, which must have continued at least a quarter hour. At last, however, it squeezed itself through an opening and was gone.

Here and there a bird would dart from the wall, always away in a straight line so that there was hardly time to see it. Within minutes of its relief and release it was, one supposes, far out over the open ocean.

The silent swirling of birds all about us continued for over an hour, but now it was getting lighter and the numbers were diminishing. By 2:15 the changing of the guard at the Broch of Mousa was over. Now one would never guess that inside this stone wall was life, that hearts were beating in there. Even the whirring watchworks had stopped.

After we had climbed a hill to see the sunset blossom again, now as sunrise, we returned over the moors to the broch. There it stood in the flooding new light, a monument for tourists, like the Castle of Edinburgh, if it had been accessible to them. One could imagine the official guide, with his patter about the ways of Picts and the features of their architecture, leading his flock through it. The chattering sightseers, and the silent but breathing life hidden in the stone, would still be as far apart as if the former had been in their home towns, the latter skimming the troughs of the mid-Atlantic. Implausible ghosts of reality from an alien world would be listening to tourists, inches away, who could have no inkling of their presence. In the full and disenchanting daylight, however, it was no longer credible that there was a whole strange world of birds inside this dead and silent wall.

Nevertheless, we pursued a certain investigation we had planned. Near the broch, at two separate points where time had crumbled down a stone wall to less than two feet high, we had the previous evening heard the snoring signal. Now, at the first of these points, we lifted off one stone after another until we could see, in a dark recess at ground level, a white egg on a circular bed of grasses. It seemed too large for the egg of so small a bird, and there was no room in the recess, as far as we could see, for a parent bird to be hiding. Touching the egg, however, we found it warm.

Then, while I was setting up tripod and camera for a photographic record, a faint clucking-clicking sound made me turn my eyes to the recess, where a Storm Petrel, a couple of feet from my face, was moving out of nowhere to cover the egg. It settled down and sat watching me.

At the other point along the wall, when the last stone was lifted from over its head, the sitting bird remained on its one large egg, which could be seen under its tail.

After photography we rebuilt the wall over the two sitting birds, each of which remained apparently undisturbed as we posed the stones over it. We belonged to an incomprehensible outer world that they could hardly recognize.

Storm Petrels, by contrast with swallows, know as little of us men as we know of Storm Petrels, by contrast with our knowledge of swallows. I was struck by the fact that they made no move to defend themselves, as other birds do. Even the one we held in our hands did not bite our fingers, and there was no threatening gesture like opening the bill. A larger relative, the Fulmar, which roosts on commanding positions all over Shetland, opens wide its bill to eject a malodorous orange fluid in the direction of any intruder. Storm Petrels, according to the literature, should do likewise, but these did not.

Another observation was of the cleanness of the two nests. We saw little trace of droppings such as one finds in the nests of other species. Since nesting Storm Petrels may go for days without food, even the nestlings, it may be that there is not the same problem of fouling their nests.

The sense of mystery in man is, in the first instance, only an expression of his own ignorance; but secondarily it may be the expression of how great, beyond human comprehension, the world is. Most of us are so preoccupied with our own immediate lives and surroundings that, especially if we live only in cities, we are unaware of all the time and space beyond. There are urgent and wholly absorbing questions of politics, of economic production and trade, of social strife. Philosophers who could well have been born in the cafés of Paris, where they spend their lives, proclaim the doctrine that the world is man's world, that he is the sole creator of any order in it. They can see that this is so by simply looking about them, just as the bee that remains in the hive can, by looking about, see that what it inhabits is a bee-made world.

The Storm Petrel knows our human world only incidentally and along its outermost fringes. In the wide oceans by day and night it sometimes sees a ship passing and follows it, as it would follow a whale, for what it finds in its wake; or it sees an airplane crossing from horizon to horizon; but I would guess that it attaches as little importance to them as the philosopher does to the world outside the city. It knows nothing about man's creation of the world. In its view, the land areas of the earth, on which man works his will, constitute mere rim for the one great ocean that envelops the globe. Even where the birds of Mousa nest, skuas must seem more important than men.

Nevertheless, there is an association, however tenuous. Thousands of years ago, men whom the Parisian philosopher must acknowledge as his forerunners built the abandoned bastion in which these insignificant creatures of the wild continue secretly, year after year, to bring forth their new generations, before they return to the untrodden ocean that, if they were philosophers, they would proclaim as the one and only reality.

Sun, wind, and cloud
    shall fail not from the face of it,
Stinging, ringing spindrift,
    nor the fulmar flying free.

—KIPLING

II. THE FULMAR FLYING FREE

IF THE Storm Petrel is the least conspicuous of the birds that nest in Shetland, its relative the Fulmar is the most conspicuous. One of the medium-sized members of the order *Procellariiformes*, it is, loosely speaking, a small albatross—and that is what it looks like.

Guides to bird-identification say that, superficially, it is like a gull. The word "superficially" should be emphasized, however, because it is quite unlike a gull to the eye of any practiced observer. As a flying machine, especially, it belongs to an altogether different category. It is a projectile rather than a parachute, adapted to swift rather than drifting flight.

The wings of most large birds, although they must be capable of flapping, are also designed for sailing on the wind, letting it do the work. In sailing flight, the greater the air-speed the less wing-surface is needed or desirable. The Fulmar, by this test, is a bird for high winds. Like albatrosses, and like airplanes designed primarily for speed, it has wings that, by their narrowness, have a proportionately smaller surface than those, for example, of gulls. Fulmars are not at all adapted to floating on offshore breezes, as gulls are, but they ride with ease the roaring storms of mid-ocean, storms in which gulls, with wings half folded, would still be buffeted and tossed. The range and rate of their travels, which may take them right across the Atlantic, depend on steady gale-winds deflected upward from the running combers that mount with the lapse of time and the extension of the wind's reach. Like witches on broomsticks, the Fulmars ride the tempest back and forth across the oceans, but are relatively confined when the weather is what gulls or men would call good.

The body of the Fulmar in flight is cylindrical, the large round head integral with it as if there were no neck at all. The wings appear to be attached to this tubular fuselage, not high-up like the wings of gulls, but halfway down. In sailing flight they extend out stiffly like laths. A gull's wing, by contrast, is flexible along its length, with a conspicuous articulation. Broad at its base, its leading edge curves gracefully from the body up to a projecting joint, beyond which it sweeps back again in another curve to the wingtip. This is a wing for hanging, drifting, and circling lazily in uncertain breezes, not for riding gales.

The tail of the Fulmar is short and broad. It twists and bends to keep the sailplane, of which it is an appendage, balanced and on course. Its shortness, providing little surface, shows it to be a rudder for high winds.

The superficial resemblance to a gull is confined virtually to color. The same size as our Ring-billed Gull, the typical Atlantic Fulmar has the same white body and gray mantle (as the upper surface of wings and back is called). But the mantle has a silvery-blue sheen when the plumage is fresh, and the tail, rather than being white like those of gulls, is a dull gray on its upper and under surfaces alike. In the white head, so large and round as to remind one, in flight, of the Snowy Owl, its eyes appear black and far larger than those of any gull. Their extraordinary size, however, is an illusion produced by patches of black feathers at their inner corners. The Fulmar's bill, in its shortness, contributes to the owl-like impression made by the head. It is simply a stubby variety of the heavy hooked albatross bill, the nostrils set in a tube on top.

The Fulmar, by contrast with the gulls, belongs to an order of primitive and small-brained birds. Almost all the species of birds that live their lives in the open sea, except when they resort to land for breeding, have the reputation of being stupid. It may not be without foundation. When persecuted by man, many of these birds seem unaware of what is happening, make little or no attempt to escape, and hardly defend themselves. On land and even on the water they can often be picked up in the hand, or snared by dropping a noose over the head, or fished up on a line, or killed with sticks; and no amount of experience seems to put them on guard. Consequently, the traditional names by which sailors know them are generally associated with stupidity. Members of the *Procellariiformes* are "gonies," a vernacular term for simpleton, or "mollymawks," from a Dutch term that means foolish gull. Similarly, the tropical species of the Gannet's family (*Sulidae*) are "boobies."

I speculate that seabirds may be less intelligent than land birds because the environment with which they have to cope offers less variety. An albatross spends its whole life among the swells and running waves of an ocean that changes little over thousands of miles, feeding on such organic matter as floats freely upon its surface. It nests on the sands of desert islands where, as a rule, there are no predators requiring the development of cunning in defence. How different is the life of a crow or a parrot, both notable for their intelligence, or that of any land bird at all! The typical gulls, as well, rather than being truly pelagic like albatross and Fulmar, are birds of offshore, inshore, or inland waters.

Not only in space, but also in time, the environment to which seabirds belong is relatively invariable. The ocean, which is much the same on one side of the globe as on the other, is also much the same now as it was three thousand years ago, when an Odysseus, legendary or real, sailed upon its "unharvested" waters. This alone would account for the fact that the orders of birds that inhabit the sea are, for the most part, so much more primitive, so much less developed on the evolutionary scale, than the orders of birds that inhabit the land. They have not had to evolve as the land birds have to meet a changing environment.

I began by observing that the Fulmar, which has now become the most abundant seabird of the northern hemisphere, is the most conspicuous of all the birds that nest in Shetland. My impression is that the entire archipelago—all coastline, with no point in it as much as three miles from the sea—has become virtually a single colony of Fulmars. This is extraordinary when one considers that the first nesting on record occurred in 1878. In the breeding season it is ubiquitous. Most of the little ledges and pockets of every bluff and cliff, where they are not solidly pre-empted by other cliff-nesters, are occupied by one or a couple of Fulmars. They roost on peat banks, on the faces of cuts bordering automobile roads, on the chimney-pots of crofts, on mediaeval or prehistoric ruins like those of Jahrlshof and Mousa. Everywhere and all the time one sees them in flight, traversing the moors back and forth, patrolling the cliffs, sweeping the bays and sounds. They appear to be evenly distributed over the sea—generally birds in flight pursuing each its individual way—as far as I have gone from Shetland on its surface (which is all the way to Aberdeen). They don't actually flock at sea, in my experience, but sometimes by the density of their numbers they tend to become one indefinitely spread-out conglomeration extending to the limits of vision in every direction.

The first Fulmar I ever saw (and it was less than two months ago as I write) was on my way to Shetland, from the window of a train that was running along the North Sea coast after having crossed the Firth of Forth. In the next two weeks I was to acquire such familiarity with these birds as generally comes only with lifelong intimacy. Their ubiquity was only one reason for this. The other was that one could observe them, whether roosting or in flight, at the closest range. Many birds roosting in accessible positions could be taken up in the hand, if one was prepared to cope with the unpleasant method of defence that I am about to describe. And one had only to station oneself at the top of almost any cliff in order to have the projectiles pass, repeatedly, so close that one could almost reach out and touch them.

Fulmars are not notably respectful of men. If a man approaches a roosting bird that is not sitting tightly it will drop from its roost and fly away. However, when he comes right up to a bird that is not of a mind to leave, it is likely to start working its throat as if gathering saliva. Next it may suddenly open its bill wide and eject in his direction, from deep in its throat, a stream of what looks like reddish tobacco-juice. This habit of spitting, widespread among the members of its order, is apparently the Fulmar's primary defence.

I have seen it used with effect by one Fulmar against another that was preparing to land alongside it on a roosting ledge which it evidently intended to keep for itself, although in this context it may properly be regarded as threat-display rather than active defence.

The Venables, authors of that exemplary book, *Birds and Mammals of Shetland*, report that "we have several times seen fulmars, or even a single fulmar, feeding on carrion while great black-backs and bonxies stood back waiting their turn." Knowing the predatory aggressiveness and strength of the bonxie (as the Great Skua is locally called), a substantially bigger bird than the Fulmar, I can only conclude that the latter's mode of defence is effective in eliciting the respect of birds that might otherwise dispose of it at a stroke—as the Great Black-backed Gull could too. When I recall how effective the similar defence of skunks is, it seems to me remarkable that more species have not, in their evolution, developed it.

Observing the Shetland Fulmars at the height of their breeding season, one soon discovered that a large proportion of the birds occupying and defending nesting sites on the cliffs did not really have nests or eggs or young. They were simply "playing house," as children do. Later I learned from James Fisher's classic monograph that those under the age of sexual maturity (and no one knows at what age it comes) will year after year go through this make-believe, even to the extent of incubating stones that serve as play eggs. This seems a wasteful use of what, at least in terms of any single colony, appears to be limited nesting space.

There are other puzzles. One is that each year the birds start returning to their breeding colonies and taking up their nesting sites as early as November, although the first eggs are not laid before late spring or early summer. Another is that a large proportion of the Fulmars spend their time and energy, at the height of the breeding season, incessantly patrolling the cliffs. Each individual takes a limited area as its beat, along which it follows the highly irregular contour of the cliff as closely as possible, going in and out with every recess and protuberance until, arrived at the end of

its beat, it sweeps away from the cliff and back in a
half circle to resume the patrol. I don't know how
long any individual keeps this kind of thing up, but
the cliffs are everywhere constantly patrolled. The
expenditure of energy seems purposeless.

The Fulmars also have a habit of sweeping upward
almost to the vertical for a landing on some steep
ledge of the cliff, but then veering off without landing
to resume their flight; or landing for a moment, tarsi
pressed against the slope, perhaps shuffling upward
with wings half extended and wavering, only to fall
off again and resume flight. At often as not, the reason
for the apparent change of mind is the hostile reaction
of a bird already roosting at or near the landing site.

While most of the nesting sites, real or pretend, are
occupied by only one bird, pairs are not infrequent on
them, and where one finds a pair they are often addressing each other in a ludicrous display. Its chief
element is an opening of the bill wider than one
would have thought possible. At the same time, the
two birds keep slowly twisting their heads about in
the most awkward attitudes they can manage, while
they utter rapid series of guttural grunts that give a

lugubrious character to their antics. Often a third bird will land next to a pair, thereby setting off a performance *à trois* that surpasses in solemn absurdity the lobster quadrille in *Alice in Wonderland.*

Fulmars do not stand up on their webbed toes like gulls and ducks. Rather, like loons and grebes they rest on the whole length of their tarsi. Loons and grebes have no choice in the matter because their legs, adapted primarily for surface diving and underwater swimming, are placed so far back on their bodies. But Fulmars do not ordinarily dive or swim underwater, and they can stand up on their toes if they want to. The utility to them of having the whole tarsus in contact with the ground becomes evident when one sees them landing and moving about on the cliffs and turfy bluffs where they habitually roost. The tarsus thereby braces the bird against a surface that, in its steepness, may approach the vertical. Gulls, which perch and perambulate on level ground, could not cling at all to the slopes on which Fulmars roost or make their shuffling way. (Storm Petrels, which likewise have no occasion to land on level ground but must be able to cling to steep slopes or vertical stone faces at their nesting sites, also perch on the whole tarsus.) In excitement, however, Fulmars do momentarily rise up on their toes, either partly or entirely.

I have never seen the Fulmar in a gale at sea, when it presumably flies like its relatives the shearwaters (which I have seen). Close to the massively shifting surface, often hidden in the troughs, it tilts up first on one wing-tip, then the other, to conform to the gradient of the traveling wave along which it sweeps. It adapts itself to the wave's inclination.

In Shetland I became familiar with its flight over gentle or moderate seas, when it alternates a series of stiff wingbeats with a glide on rigidly set wings. The bird rises and falls in an undulating trajectory that does not vary. Its glide begins as it approaches the bottom of each undulation, continues through the dip and on into the rise until it is almost spent, when the wings resume their stiff beating as the bird goes over the top and down the other side.

I have also seen it on calm water, but against a brisk breeze, rise from a floating position to run over the surface for a short distance with pattering feet, its wings extended but motionless. A like habit in some of the storm-petrel family is said to account for the appellation "petrel," in allusion to Peter's performance in *Matthew* 14:29.

Stiff-winged though it is, the Fulmar can neverthe-less exhibit a spectacular dexterity in flight when, moving with its usual momentum, it follows in and out the broken contours of the Shetland cliffs. The basic process of its flight, even in these circumstances, is that of the alternation between gliding and wing-beating; but it is constantly having to check itself or veer, twisting its tail strenuously, apparently even using the webbed feet which extend along either side of the tail to help in the steering. These operations often have to be performed abruptly to prevent col-lisions between birds patrolling in opposite directions. I have seen Fulmars, when suddenly struck by an upward gust, check themselves with wings upthrown and tail cocked like a wren's to prevent being blown aloft.

(I am tempted to digress, here, with a general note. The observational processes of birds, and their physical responses, must operate with a rapidity far in excess of our own, so that what is fast motion to us is slow motion to them. The evidence of the speeding Fulmars that veer off from collision courses matches that of the Goshawk, a large bird that threads its way at top speed through the confusion of branches in dense woods. Near me, as I write, is a cage containing some small finches. It has a swing that they land on, even when it is in violent motion back and forth, as if it were a stationary perch. The explanation must be that to them its motion, too fast for my own eye, appears as it would to me in a slow-motion film. The bird, in terms of its own observation, hangs in the air with wings waving; it waits for the approaching bar of the swing, over which, when it comes, it simply closes its toes. If this is so, then a bird must see human beings moving at a snail's pace, must find the sun so slow in its trajectory that in its universe the length of the day is equivalent to perhaps a week in ours, and may live the equivalent of a full human life in a tenth the time.)

Let me return, now, to the relative changelessness of the seabirds' environment, which generally requires less adaptiveness of them than of land birds; for the Fulmar, in these terms, presents a paradox that makes it, in its present status, unique among birds.

When we say that man is transforming the surface of the earth, replacing its natural wilderness by his civilization, we do not have in mind the two-thirds that is ocean. It is the birds and beasts of the land that we think of as now facing the challenge of adaptation to a man-made world. With some of these species such adaptation has already been accomplished by man's own initiative in domesticating them, partly or wholly. Examples are the Rock Dove, which has become the domestic pigeon, and the Mute Swan, which lives unconfined but in dependence on man's care and provisioning over most of Europe. Others have already adapted themselves and have profited by their association with man, the outstanding example being that of the House Sparrow, which from its original home in the Nile Valley and the Middle East has accompanied the spread of human civilization around the globe. The Starling, the Chimney Swift, and the Collared Dove are other examples of obviously successful adaptation, the latter being now engaged in rapidly taking up its residence in all the cities of Europe.

Among other large birds that have adapted themselves in like manner one could name various kites of the genus *Milvus* and the American Black Vulture, which is at home in the city-streets of tropical America. Other examples are provided by the gulls that have become the scavengers of man's harbors and waterways, profiting by the refuse with which he fills them to increase their numbers.

Many birds, on the other hand, have failed or are failing to adapt themselves. There are those that have already become extinct and some that are disappearing, the number of the latter catastrophically increased in our day by the new pesticides that poison the land.

The fewest species remain unaffected, still, by man's conquest of the earth's land surface, now nearing completion. There are those that inhabit remnants of wilderness, representing nature's last resistance to man's occupation: species endemic in arctic ice-fields and tundra, in dwindling islands of rain-forest or cloud-forest, and in some desert areas.

When the count of all these has been taken, however, we still have left the birds that spend all their lives in the vast ranges of the ocean, where man is hardly present at all. Even though they must come to land periodically to breed, human civilization has been less of an obstacle to this than one might have expected. It has destroyed one species, the flightless Great Auk, and has caused serious disturbance, at least, to others on which men have preyed, but many have enjoyed a reasonable safety on uninhabited shores in the arctic or antarctic, on desert islands, on isolated sandbanks, or along the unchanged cliffs and bluffs that bound lands remodeled by man for his habitation. Many, like the Storm Petrel, have found security by remaining, when on land, in hidden cavities that they approach or leave only under cover of darkness. Moreover, even though the human population has been spreading so rapidly all over the earth, it is withdrawing from remote islands everywhere. The population of Shetland, for example, has been diminishing rapidly as part of the worldwide movement of people from rural areas to the new urban conglomerations.

This is not to say, however, that life in the great oceans has been unaffected by man. As on land, some of it has been destroyed and some of it benefited. The great whales have been destroyed. The Fulmar has been benefited. The Fulmar, in fact, provides a unique demonstration of how human activities can transform what appears to be as remote from them (and here I choose my example with an intention that will become clear) as the life of the Storm Petrel, referred to in the last chapter, is from the political maneuvers of officials in Buenos Aires.

In recent years the term "population explosion" has come into general use to denote the spectacular multiplication of the human population over the past couple of centuries, a multiplication still continuing at an ever-increasing pace. There is one other species of vertebrate, and one only, that has concurrently been experiencing a like explosion. James Fisher reports that "the fulmar has been increasing . . . by geometrical progression for two hundred years"—to which he adds: "There is only one other known animal that has been doing anything like this: man."

The fulmars of the world are divided into three populations and two species, one antarctic and the other arctic. The antarctic species (*Fulmarus glacial-oides*) represents the original population in its original range. The arctic species (*F. glacialis*) is descended from colonists of this population that, roaming beyond their normal range, found in the arctic conditions similar to those in their antarctic homes, and consequently settled there. The two northern populations that ensued, one about the northern reaches of the Atlantic and the other about the northern reaches of the Pacific, are distinguished by the taxonomists as two races, *glacialis* and *rodgersii* respectively.

There is a certain plausibility in the fact that the Fulmar originated in the southern hemisphere; for the southern hemisphere, because it is all one ocean with intrusive land-masses, is richer in seabirds than the northern hemisphere, in which the proportion of land to sea is far higher. The order *Procellariiformes*, greatest of the seabird orders in the number and variety of its species, must have originated in the southern ocean, where it still has its greatest abundance.

I speak loosely when I say that the two fulmar species are respectively antarctic and arctic, for their traditional ranges overspread into subantarctic, subarctic, and high temperate latitudes. We shall see that the expansion of the northern species has necessarily involved its southward spread, if only because there has been so little place for it to expand farther north. It is the most northerly of all birds, in the sense that it has been recorded farther north than any other, at 86°35′ N—that is, 236 land miles from the pole. The northernmost breeding colony of Fulmars found so far is in Franz Josef Land, 567 land miles from the pole.

"The whole astonishing business of the North Atlantic fulmar's spread," James Fisher writes, "has its apparent origin in Iceland." The first mention of the species on record is in an Icelandic saga that dates from the period A.D. 1000-1200. Nevertheless, in the middle of the seventeenth century there was still only

one nesting colony in Iceland. It was a century later
when the Icelandic population began to expand at a
geometric rate, so that by the middle of the present
century it came, at last, to constitute a web of colonies,
155 of them, that embraces virtually the entire Icelandic coastline.

The Fulmar spread out from Iceland at the same
time, and one of the directions in which it spread was
southeast. It crossed the intervening three hundred
miles to breed in the Faroe Islands, probably between
1816 and 1839. It first bred in Shetland, some two
hundred miles farther on, in 1878. It then spread
southward to the Orkneys and along the coasts of
mainland Britain at an accelerating pace until, by the
middle of the present century, it had closed the ring
on Britain, colonizing the south coast of England. It
has now crossed the Channel to nest on the coast of
Brittany. (On the west side of the Atlantic it still does
not breed south of a point fairly far up the coast of
Labrador.)

Virtually the only geographical irregularity in this
Icelandic saga is that the Fulmar had established itself
as a breeding bird on the remote island of St. Kilda in
the Outer Hebrides (but nowhere else in Britain) by

1697. Today, still, it dominates St. Kilda, now uninhabited by man, which provides it with a uniquely
spectacular setting. James Fisher combines the aus-
terity of the scientific attitude with a rhapsodic poetry
when he comes to give his account of the Fulmar on
this ancient breeding ground. Having said that St.
Kilda, with its great cliffs, has to be seen to be believed,
he conscientiously qualifies this in a footnote to take
account of those who have seen and still not believed.
A few paragraphs further on he writes that: "All day,
at the tops of all cliffs, the pale albatrosses of St. Kilda
play, and sway on the up-winds. From the Atlantic they
slant their way a thousand feet up to their nests; at the
level of these they become sail-planes and swing along
the cliff-top, visiting their neighbours and watching
them with cold dark eyes." This is reminiscent of some
of the writing in Homer's *Odyssey*.

Our own species, in its own population explosion,
has almost surely caused the parallel explosion of this
species relatively so remote from it. Its traditional food
had been plankton (a term that embraces all the free-
floating animal life in the seas, from microscopic
organisms to crustacea of some size) and offal, including carrion. When, in the eighteenth century, the
development of whaling began to project whaling ships
around the world and into the remotest oceans, the
Fulmars found a new supply of food that caused them
to remain in attendance on those ships, sharing in
the oil and fat provided by the dead whales that were
drawn up alongside them for flensing. The limit on
the supply of food, hitherto the only limiting factor on
the population, was suddenly removed.

The way in which man exploited the great whales,
however, beginning in the eighteenth century, brought
about their virtual extermination, so that only vestigial
populations now remain. Consequently, the great days
of whaling were over by the second half of the nineteenth century, and with them this new source of food

as a basis for the explosion of the Fulmar populations.

As whaling declined, however, a new source of unlimited food arose in the new practice of trawling. The Fulmars began to accompany the trawling fleets, surrounding the ships, when the catches were being hauled in and cleaned, in such numbers that they formed almost solid rafts about them. There are photographs of trawlers that appear to be caught in Fulmar packs as they might be in pack-ice.

If this explanation of the Fulmar's population explosion, put forward by James Fisher with the authority of so much hard research and intelligent deduction, is valid, then the future of the species is as uncertain as that of our own. It has come to depend for the maintenance of anything like its present numbers on economic activities of our own that, in the form in which we have recently been carrying them out, are temporary only. The Fulmar, like all the other species of vertebrates (and not only vertebrates), still faces the challenge of adapting itself to a human civilization, worldwide, that is in a stage of explosively unstable transition—to what, no one knows. Here we see how true this is even of birds that range the open oceans, out of sight of the land, although there has been no visible change in those oceans over thousands of years. No *visible* change, I say, but the great whales (still plentiful in my own childhood) are gone, and out of sight fundamental changes have taken place or are impending. The Baltic Sea has already been dangerously polluted by the pesticide called DDT, entering it through the rivers that drain the land on all sides; and the pollution is spreading in the Atlantic. Vast studies have now been undertaken in the United States for harvesting the oceans in ways that they have hitherto been unharvested, and even for establishing cities of men in or upon their depths.

It is true that the impact of human civilization on the natural life of the sea is still much less than its impact on the natural life of the land. Because it is less direct and less visible, however, it appears less than it really is. Let me give an example.

The only major predator to which the Fulmar has been subject since we have had knowledge of it is our own species. In Iceland and in Faroe, for many years, the natives took young Fulmars from their nests by tens of thousands each year, salting them away as reserve supplies of food. This is the background for the circumstances I am about to relate.

Those of us who are old enough must remember the psittacosis scare of the 1930s. Psittacosis is one of the few diseases of birds (identified at the time only with parrots and consequently named after their family) that are communicable to man in the form of serious illness. Epidemics of it that broke out among human beings in the United States and Europe at the beginning of the 1930s provoked emergency legislation against the importation of pet parrots, as I found out in 1934, when I tried to bring a pet parrot of my own back to the States from Guatemala. Investigation has since suggested that the epidemics were exported from Argentina. James Fisher puts the matter rather cryptically when he writes: "In 1929 in the Argentine a serious epidemic of psittacosis broke out among a large number of captive parrots, mostly of the genus *Amazona*. Under the health regulations of Argentina it was found profitable to export about five thousand parrots—mostly sick—to Europe by the first ships available. Thus the disease was introduced into Europe. . . ." It is a plausible speculation that parrots freshly dead from psittacosis were tossed overboard from some of the ships and were eaten by Faroe Fulmars (Fulmars follow ships), which thereby contracted the disease. In time it spread to Fulmar colonies in Iceland as well. Psittacosis then began to break out seasonally among those persons in Faroe and Iceland who engaged in the cleaning and salting away of the annual crop of nestling Fulmars. When the connection between the disease and the occupation was discovered, the harvesting of young Fulmars was abruptly stopped by legislation in both countries.

What the possible consequences were and are for the Fulmar populations is uncertain. When the harvesting of young Fulmars was stopped in Iceland, the harvesting of Fulmar eggs, hitherto forbidden in the interest of maintaining the crop of young Fulmars, was begun; and this is probably a more destructive form of exploitation. On the other hand, in Faroe, wherever the population of a Fulmar colony may have increased because the taking of the young had been stopped, the increased population density that ensued may have made it more vulnerable to the spread and the depredations of psittacosis, now a permanently established epizootic disease of northern Fulmars.

This history dramatizes the degree to which casual human decisions may have consequences that are both remote and beyond the scope of the foreseeable. If it is correct, as we may take it to be in its essentials, then the fundamental conditions affecting the lives of birds that inhabit oceans bordering the arctic were permanently altered when they contracted a new disease by contact with South American parrots; and they contracted the disease because certain governmental authorities were trying to deal in the most profitable way with the outbreak of a disease among pet parrots for which there was an as yet unsuspecting market in a faraway part of the world.

Our planet has at last become one world of interconnected life, and even a "fulmar flying free" in the changeless wastes of the ocean, far from any habitation of man, cannot expect to remain unaffected by what occurs in a human settlement, even though what occurs is a minor incident and the settlement is seven thousands miles away across the unbroken and unharvested sea.

Great
Black-backed Gull

Lesser
Black-backed Gull

Herring Gull

Common Gull

Kittiwake

Black-headed
Gull

And the first man who walked the cliffs of Rame,

As I this year, looked down and saw the same

Blotches of rusty red on ledge and cleft

With gray-green spots on them while right and left

A dizzying tangle of gulls were floating and flying

Wheeling and crossing and darting, crying and crying. —J. C. SQUIRE

III. OF GULLS AND MEN

IN THE evolution of life on earth there has been a gradual separation of forms descended from common ancestors, and it is convenient to indicate degree of separation by some system of categories, necessarily arbitrary, such as that of orders, families, genera, and species. These categories, however, do not exist in nature; they are the inventions of man. The existential reality, as it is actually found in nature, can be fitted to them easily in some cases, in others only by straining. For example, there is no difficulty in grouping the penguins as one distinct order; and, varied though the *Procellariiformes* are, they have certain evident traits in common that also distinguish them from all other forms.

One large grouping of birds, however, about which the taxonomists have appeared uncertain is that which includes the gulls. Should there be a single order into which the gulls, terns, and skuas, the shorebirds (sandpipers, plovers, etc.), and the auks (guillemots, puffins, etc.) are all lumped together; or should there be three separate orders? The layman like myself is not qualified to take part in the discussion of these matters. What appears to be generally accepted is that, within whatever larger grouping, the gulls, terns, and skuas, at least, belong together. All three actively impose their presence on the attention of visitors to Shetland.

Wherever, on this aquaterrestrial globe, land and water meet, the gulls occupy a dominant position. The typical genus, comprising almost all the species, is *Larus*. It appears to be an unusually plastic genus, having evolved a great variety of forms to fit the variety of habitats, all over the earth, where land and water meet. There are gulls adapted to life in the waters of the continental shelves, others adapted to estuaries and brackish backwaters, others to inland ponds and watercourses. They range in size from the Little Gull, eleven inches long, to the Great Black-backed Gull, over twenty-seven inches long; yet both these species and the thirty-five or so in-between have the distinctiveness of their kind, being immediately recognizable as gulls.

An idea of how complete and yet distinctive the gamut of gulls is may be had by looking at the plate in Peterson's *Field Guide to Western Birds* that juxtaposes in descending order of size five species native to the Pacific coast of North America. From the Glaucous-winged to the Short-billed, they appear as essentially the same bird in five different sizes. Another group within the genus, which wears a dark hood in the breeding season, consists of some fifteen species varying from the Great Black-headed Gull of central Asia, almost the size of the Great Black-back, down to the Little Gull. The varieties of Herring Gull and Lesser Black-back intergrade to such an extent, forming a nearly continuous gamut, that the taxonomists are sometimes embarrassed in their efforts to distinguish individual species. This is true, as well, of the forms intermediate between the Herring and the Iceland Gull: Thayer's Gull and Kumlien's.

The plasticity of the genus seems to be matched by

the adaptability of its species to changing environments. Formerly, natural changes, like those associated
with the successive ice-ages, occurred over tens of
thousands of years. In terms of such a time-scale, the
present spread of human civilization, transforming the
earth, is an explosion. The consequent challenge to
varieties of birds and beasts that were adapted to a
natural world has been to make a new life for themselves in the new and still changing environment, and
to make it at a rate that largely precludes the process
of fundamental genetic adaptation. The gulls have been
among those whose response to this challenge, so far
from representing a rear-guard defence, has been to
profit by it.[1] They have fitted themselves into our human
civilization, generally playing an indispensable role as
scavengers of its waterways, and they are, in consequence, vastly increasing their numbers over wide
areas. Some of the dominant species are undergoing
population explosions similar to those of the Fulmar
and our own species. K. H. Voous reports, for example,
that a population of some ten thousand nesting pairs of
Herring Gulls in the Netherlands between 1925 and
1930 had grown to at least thirty thousand by 1940.
The adaptability of this species is shown by the fact
that it has taken to nesting on the roofs of buildings. I
recall a dinner at a restaurant on the top floor of a
skyscraper in Stockholm throughout which one perched
three feet away from our table, albeit separated by a
glass window, watching us eat. In the crowded harbor
of Lerwick, Shetland, these great birds perch on the
decks of the fishing boats, amid the tangled gear and
cordage, while the men clean fish, ready to snatch any
discarded morsel. In Geneva the Black-headed Gulls

[1] "Gulls originally seem to have been quite rare in London,
where in mediaeval times the main bird scavengers seem to
have been kites and corvids. Apparently the gulls first started to
spread up the Thames immediately after the passage of local
bird protection Acts in the 1880s. . . ."—Bourne

forage with the pigeons in the streets, and come to the windows of apartment houses to be fed by hand.

The adaptability of the gulls, however, is only half the explanation of their successful adjustment to our civilization. No less essential is their acceptance by us, and their consequent exemption from the genocide to which we are subjecting some species.

As poignant an example as any of adaptable species rejected by man are many of the ducks, geese, and swans. In waters enclosed by crowded cities, where hunting must be forbidden for the protection of the human population—the port of Geneva, for example, or the Zürich River—wild ducks become as tame as barnyard fowl; but outside such waters they are the victims of pursuit by a small minority of men for whom hunting is a passion. The dwindling remnants of the once-great flocks of geese that migrate to central and southern Europe every winter can find no place to come down without danger of being shot. Everywhere the gunners stand in wait for them.

The gulls, then, in addition to having the ability to accept our civilization, have also had the indispensable good fortune to be accepted by it.

I venture here several generalizations, not necessarily without exceptions, illustrated by the *Larus* gulls that nest in Shetland and are common there. These gulls, in descending order of size, are the Great Black-back, the Herring, the Lesser Black-back (virtually the same size as the Herring), the so-called Common Gull, and the Black-headed Gull.

One generalization is that the larger the species of *Larus* the more it is associated with open salt-water, although remaining coastal. The medium-size species are generally more at home in the brackish water of estuaries (as witness the respective habitats of our

American Herring and Ring-billed Gulls). The small species are associated with rivers and fresh-water lakes in the interior. This generalization undoubtedly represents a logic on which it would be interesting to speculate.

Another general rule, which must also represent a logic, is that the larger species have proportionately heavier bills, those of the smaller being shorter, more slender, more delicate. (I rather think the case is the same among other groups of birds.) This is of great help in field identification—for example, in distinguishing between such species as the Herring and Common Gulls—since nothing is more deceptive as a criterion in field identification than the apparent overall size of a bird, which varies with the setting and circumstances in which it is seen.

Finally, I record my impression that, in flight, the larger the gull the longer it seems in the part that projects beyond the wings. When all three species are circulating together in the sky I have seen how the Great Black-backs appear long-necked, especially when crying with bills strained upward, as they so often are; how the Herring Gulls give the same impression much less markedly; and how the Common Gulls give it not at all. If this is a valid observation, and if there is a reason for everything in nature, then there is a reason for this too.

It appears to be in keeping with the first of my generalizations that, in Shetland, the Great Black-backs have their nesting colonies on top of those small but high islands, called "stacks," which have broken away from the immediately adjacent cliffs of the main shoreline; that the Herrings have theirs on slopes and bluffs at the edge of the sea, or on the neighboring moors; that the Common Gulls are apt to have theirs farther inland on the moors; and that the Black-heads, smallest of all, have theirs among the reeds that border fresh-water pools in the inland peat bogs.

All five species swoop with great crying and commotion at the human intruder in their nesting colonies, but not coming as close to him or attacking with such fierceness and power as the terns and skuas on which I shall be reporting further on.

In a nesting colony of Herring Gulls, two well-developed fledglings that ran before me at the top of a steep bluff got themselves caught in a chicken-wire fence that had been put up to confine sheep. One of them managed, at last, to free itself, but the other got so badly entangled that I had to extricate it myself. When, having done so, I let go of it, it dashed away over the edge of the bluff and thereupon found itself launched on its first flight. Its incompletely fledged wings beating, it descended several hundred feet at an angle of some forty-five degrees to splash into the sea.

What prompts me to recount this episode is that, throughout its maiden flight, this juvenile was repeatedly attacked and struck by adults of its kind. For a few seconds after it landed they continued to dive upon it, but now it was poised and could defend itself with open bill. The attackers therefore desisted and went off about their business, leaving the young bird to find out for the first time what it was to ride a great swell. I take this episode to illustrate the impulse, common to most higher animals, to attack any individual of their kind who appears to be in trouble. If a crow is injured, and other crows see that it is having a hard time flying, they will immediately mob it, driving it to the ground or to cover, perhaps killing it. There have been recent reports of how Carolina Chickadees, caught in spider-webs, were set upon by others of their kind. The impulse that this represents could plausibly be interpreted as a contribution to natural selection, or simply to the maintenance of the community's health at the expense of the individual. The elimination of the weak, although practiced indiscriminately, must often prevent the spread of disease or the propagation of genetic defects.

The same impulse may be seen to operate among boys on a playground or among men engaged in politics. In such cases, however, it stands opposed to other considerations and motives that men develop only in an advanced stage of civilization.

No one, seeing a Kittiwake for the first time, could have any hesitation in recognizing it as a gull. At first glance he might identify it as a small member of the typical genus, *Larus*; for it is typical in its white body and tail, its gray mantle, and its yellow bill. As he became more familiar with it, however, he would be impressed by certain distinctive features. Some of them might be too superficial to mark it as a separate genus: the eye is dark rather than yellow; the gray of the mantle, lacking blue, is mouse-color, and fades toward the wing-tips, which are abruptly black and without the white spots, called "mirrors," of most typical gulls. A fundamental structural characteristic is the shortness of the leg, observable only when the bird is perched on land; and this is accompanied by a feature that, although hardly noticeable in the field, is the most stressed by the taxonomists, the absence of any except a vestigial hind toe. (Hence its specific scientific name, *tridactyla.*)

Observing it on the wing, however, what strikes me as its most distinctive and fundamental feature is not mentioned in any of the literature with which I am familiar: its wings differ in form from the wings in *Larus*. They are more angled, intermediate in this between the typical gulls and the terns. From the body they project more sharply forward to the joint, from which they then rake back more sharply to a point.

This difference in the form of the wing makes a difference in manner of flight. In all large birds, wings that are for sailing flight tend to extend out straight, with little bend at the joint, as in the Fulmar, the

Turkey Vulture, or the Golden Eagle (by contrast with
the Osprey). It follows that the Kittiwake sails less
than the *Larus* species, being intermediate in this, too,
between them and the terns. For the most part it flies
with a steady wing-stroke that varies only as the flyer
shows its agility in veering and dipping. One may see a
bird in front of its nesting cliffs sweep in a half circle
on fixed wings outstretched, but this maneuver, in my
experience, is only brief and occasional. Flocks may,
for all I know, circle aloft in soaring flight, like *Larus*
gulls; but, if so, I have never seen them do it.

In addition to our one species, which is circumpolar
and abundant in large parts of its range, the genus
Rissa has one other species, the Red-legged Kittiwake,
which is confined to islands about the southern rim of
the Bering Sea. Our species is the only truly pelagic
gull, for outside the nesting season, like the Fulmar, it
roams the open oceans, generally out of sight of land,
crossing them freely. If there are gulls following one's
ship in the middle of the North Atlantic or the North
Pacific they must be Kittiwakes.

Under any circumstances the Kittiwake would be the
loveliest of gulls. Northerly as it is in its range (up to
84° 52′ N, 355 land miles from the pole), so that it
often nests among the ice-floes, and exposed as no other
gull is to the great seas and unbridled winds of the
open ocean, it still exhibits in its form all the refinement and delicacy of which nature is capable—as re-
fined as a swallow, as poised and deft in the air as a
butterfly. I suspect that it tends to remain far from
land, except in the breeding season, precisely because
it is not adapted, like the Fulmar, to riding out the great
storms. It needs as much space as possible between
itself and a lee shore, for it cannot indefinitely hold
against great gales that drive it landward. After days of
westerly gales in the Atlantic, individuals turn up as far
inland as Switzerland, where I have twice seen one on
the Lake of Geneva. If they do not similarly turn up

inland in North America, that must be because the gale-force winds of the northern hemisphere are from the west, and the Pacific, by contrast with the Atlantic, is what its name denotes.

The head of the Kittiwake appears somewhat bigger and rounder than that of other gulls, and the black eye makes the bird seem more gentle. (I don't know why it is that a yellow iris in any bird, whether a Goshawk or a Herring Gull, gives an impression of bad-tempered fierceness.) Its bill might have been fashioned by a goldsmith. Its legs appear black. They are so much shorter than those of other gulls, one guesses, because, unlike the others, it has virtually no occasion to walk over the ground; nor need it swim at a great rate when, far out at sea, it rides the waves. A flick of its wings lifts it out of the water, to put down again wherever it wishes like a feather coming to rest. The mouse-gray mantle would fade to pure white at the wing-tips if these had not been dipped in black ink. The wings of other gulls seem broad and rounded beside these, so sharp and flickering. Finally, it is not quite true that, as the books tell us, the tail of the adult is not, like that of the immature, slightly forked. Surely the adult's tail is also forked, although even more slightly, and this impression is strengthened by the fact that it is so often held in a position of lateral curvature, concave side up.

In Shetland as elsewhere the Kittiwakes nest in dense colonies on the faces of sheer cliffs—not where there are ledges of substantial depth, but along horizontal fissures or seams that appear to offer hardly more than a momentary foothold for a bird. These fissures, stretching perhaps for a couple of hundred feet or more, are one above the other, so that what one sees on the cliffs is continuous lines of nesting birds in successive rows, like the staff in a musical score. Unlike many seabirds, the Kittiwakes do not lay their eggs on the bare rock but build nests of seaweed and grass to keep their eggs from falling off; otherwise, I suppose, they could not lay eggs and raise young at all on ledges so narrow. The nests are separated only so far as the nesting birds can defend by striking with their gold bills from their respective nests. Since the eggs and young of each pair are generally two, the space between nests fills up completely as the fledglings develop, so that by mid-July one sees the inward-facing birds shoulder-to-shoulder. The developing young have no room to move about or exercise. There are always birds of other species in or around such colonies, chiefly Common Murres, but always, in my experience, on somewhat deeper ledges. And wherever there is a single niche that will accommodate a Fulmar, there a Fulmar will be found. On the broadest ledges, generally close to the sea, Shags have their nests.

In such a colony a degree of commotion is continuous. The scene is a snowstorm of flying birds coming or going, rising from below to insert themselves into the lines of nesting birds, or falling off to make for the open sea where they find their food. All this commotion is heightened by the continuous crying of the birds, producing a cumulative uproar in which one's ear can hardly distinguish the *kitti-aa-a* of each individual. Below the musical staff, as a *basso continuo*, one hears the successive roars of the ocean swells as they lift up the cliffs, splashing and foaming, only to expire and fall away again.

Sociable as they are, Kittiwakes travel nowhere alone. One sees them in streams that seem to have no beginning or end, some heading out to sea, others inland to the fresh-water lochs where they bathe communally and regale themselves. The Venables report how on the island of Foula, from which their nesting colonies are now gone, the inhabitants remembered the great flights of earlier days. "The islanders have told us," they write, "how 'the string was never broken and they were singing all the way.' The Isbisters of Leraback said that sometimes they could hardly hear themselves speak but they

did not mind; it was so 'lightsome' hearing the birds!"
(What accounts for the disappearance of these colonies
is the increase of the predatory Great Skua on Foula.)

One respect in which the Kittiwake differs from the
Larus gulls is that it is, presumably, hardly more associated with man than the Storm Petrel, and less than
the Fulmar, since it has not come to depend for its
food on man's harvesting of the sea. It is not a bird of
the edge between land and water, not a scavenger, not
(according to the literature) a frequenter of man's ports
and harbors. It was therefore with surprise that, on
July 17, 1968, I found flocks of Kittiwakes scavenging
alongside the Herring Gulls about the docks in the
harbor of Aberdeen. Amid the activity of clanging
machinery they circled about, dipping down between
boats and barges to pluck prizes from the surface of
the foul swirling waters. So delicate a bird in a setting
so human, and so alien to it!

*When man was created, it was told that he
should have dominion over the fowl of the air.
But the message was never delivered to
the Skua because he lived too far away.*

—SOUTH GEORGIA LEGEND

IV. BIRDS THAT ATTACK MEN

WE COMMONLY refer to "gulls and terns," associating them in our minds as the two branches of a single group, which the taxonomists identify as the family *Laridae*. What the genus *Larus* is to the gulls *Sterna* is to the terns. It includes the great preponderance of the species, which total some forty-five all over the world, and therefore presents itself to our minds as the typical genus.

The typical terns, like the typical gulls, have features in common that make them easily identifiable in the field, and they also constitute a gamut of species that have developed to meet a variety of environmental circumstances. Considerably smaller than gulls on the whole, terns nevertheless range in size from the Caspian Tern, almost the size of a Herring Gull, to the Least Tern, the size of a Starling.

On both the American and European coasts of the Atlantic the tern we are most familiar with is the Common Tern. To the north of its breeding range it is replaced by the closely similar Arctic Tern, which is famous for having the longest annual migration of any bird or beast. Breeding in arctic and subarctic lands, it winters in antarctic and subantarctic lands during the antarctic summer. Consequently it never experiences winter, although it must be familiar with drift ice and snow flurries at both extremes of its range. Many of its members must enjoy more hours of daylight per year than those of any other kind of life.

Just as the Fulmar we know is the descendent of Antarctic Fulmars that colonized the north, so a reverse colonization by Arctic Terns is thought to account for an almost identical species, the Antarctic Tern, whose ancestors from the north remained in the southern hemisphere and developed a more sedentary disposition.

Since none of the terns commonly land and rest on the water as gulls do, it is extraordinary that the Arctic Tern on its migrations is completely pelagic, crossing the great oceans and frequently to be seen, as I have seen it, midway between the Old World and the New. Do they keep flying all night as well as all day? Or are there enough bits of driftwood and clumps of floating seaweed to provide them with roosting sites, at least in calm weather? *The Handbook of British Birds* reports that they do not normally feed on migration, a negative assertion that it would surely be difficult to prove. Since their principal food is small fishes caught by plunging from the air, one is bound to wonder why they would practice such abstinence in the course of flights that, in some cases at least, exceed ten thousand miles.

The Arctic Tern illustrates one of the most fascinating of mysteries associated with birds. As in the case of many other species on land and sea, the young of the year undertake the southward migration weeks ahead of the adults. How do they know the traditional migration routes unless they inherit their ancestors' memory of the geography involved? The notion, however, that they do inherit knowledge that their ancestors have learned surpasses the bounds of genetic orthodoxy.

Most species of tern, including the Arctic, are airy-fairy creatures. Their tapering and pointed wings, reaching forward to the joint and then raked back, each V-shaped in silhouette, are too sharply angled for sailing flight. Nevertheless, they provide an even greater excess of surface than those of gulls, just as those of gulls have proportionately more surface than those of the Fulmar. One could say that, in normal flight, these bent wings flick with the regularity of a pulse, except that the word "flick" does not suggest the depth of each

stroke. The wings snap down in successive strokes that
rock the relatively small body between them. The bird
may remain hanging in the wind, whipping it with the
regular downbeats of its wings, forked tail spread and
outer tail-feathers streaming wide—until, seeing a fish
below, it suddenly dives vertically to pierce the water,
from which it emerges in flight a moment later, its bill
holding crosswise a shaving of silver that shimmers in
its final efforts still to swim.

Where the breeding ranges of the Common and
Arctic Terns overlap they nest together in mixed colonies, being so closely related. Since Shetland is so far
north, however, one finds no more than a scattering of
Common Terns in the large Arctic Tern colonies. While
everyone agrees on the difficulty of distinguishing the
two species from each other with certainty, I found the
greater length of the Arctic's streaming outer tail-
feathers, seen as the birds passed in flight, a convenient
basis of identification, subject to confirmation, and the

cries of the Arctic Tern were less harsh than those of the Common.

On the stony uplands of Eshaness, one sunny day, we found ourselves in the midst of a large colony with fledgling young already on the wing. The fact that young with wings and tails still only half grown could nevertheless fly freely, although beating their wings hard, shows how much excess wing-surface the adults have. The adults dove at us screaming; but such small and delicate beings could not, at first, intimidate such stalwart creatures as we were, even when they struck our heads with their wings in passing. I took a more serious view of them, however, after one struck me so hard that it was as if I had been hit in the head by a stone.

While all the larger gulls engage in some predation—
forcing other birds to surrender their prey, feeding on
the eggs and young of nesting seabirds, sometimes
killing small birds to eat them—they are not primarily
designed for the purpose. Their relatives of the family
Stercorariidae are.

It is common to refer to the world's four species of
skua as predators of the sea, the marine counterparts
of the hawks and falcons on land. This, however, blurs
the distinction between two kinds of predation: killing
for food and piracy. Although the skuas engage in both
kinds, they are primarily pirates: they attack other
seabirds to make them surrender food they have caught
for themselves. Attacking to kill is less common. They
also feed to a greater or lesser extent on fish, other
marine organisms, and offal that they find for themselves on the surface of the sea.

It is worth noting that the only other professional
predators of the sea, the frigate birds of the tropics, are
also pirates rather than hunters. By contrast, among
land birds piracy is almost unknown and predation
means killing. The only conspicuous exception is the
Bald Eagle's habit of pirating fish from the Osprey;
but this is not the eagle's primary means of gaining a
living, and it may not be a coincidence that it is associated with fish and a watery habitat.

The Great Skua is unique in its breeding range, being
an essentially antarctic species that, outside the circumpolar area of the southern hemisphere, has breeding colonies only in Iceland, Faroe, Shetland, and
Orkney. Since it ranges widely over the open oceans,
even crossing the equator, birds from both breeding
areas occasionally meet. In May 1967 a Great Skua
that had been banded as a nestling in Shetland, and
another that had been banded on the Antarctic continent, were both recovered in the Caribbean, the first 14
miles east of Georgetown, Guyana, the second off Gua-
deloupe.

A bird that ranges so rapidly over thousands of miles of sea must, one supposes, be capable of swift and unlabored flight, like the Fulmar; and one that makes its living by overtaking other birds in the air must be capable of bursts of speed beyond the ordinary. It is a paradox, then, that the impression the Great Skua makes on anyone who sees it at sea is of a heavy bird with labored flight. Its body is the length of a Herring Gull's, but corpulent. Again, its wings are essentially those of a gull, but seem broader; it flaps them more frequently and more heavily than any gull of comparable size. It is dark, as befits a pirate, appearing black against sea or sky, with a white flash across each wing toward the tip. (Those other pirates, the frigate birds, are also dark, and since this is exceptional among large seabirds one may speculate that there is a biological association between piracy and somber plumage.) Finally, its tail is short. The total impression is one of power rather than speed or grace. Among other seabirds it is like a heavy truck among sport cars.

The impression of power is not mistaken. When one sees this dark marauder, as so often in Shetland, standing on the brow of a hill, its stalwartness is striking.

The two posts of its legs appear wide apart, in keeping with the excessive breadth of its body. By comparison with this body, the head appears smaller than those of the gulls, but it is armed with a heavy hooked bill.

The massive breadth of the body represents the exceptional size and strength of the pectoral muscles that work the wings. This, presumably, is what makes possible such bursts of power-flight as enable the pirate to overtake other birds that one would have thought swifter as well as more elegant. It also makes it possible for it to carry off chunks of food heavier than itself. The Great Skua may, by valid criteria, have the greatest strength and stamina of any bird in the world.

On July 6, with Mr. Bob Tulloch in his motor-launch, as we were crossing Colgrave Sound to the island of Fetlar we saw a Great Skua overtake a Gannet and seize its tail-feathers in its beak. Thereupon both birds fell some thirty feet to the water, where they fought each other for about a minute, thrashing about, churning up the water, flailing with their wings. Then they broke apart to float peaceably, as it seemed, side by side. That was the last we saw of them, but Mr. Tulloch, an experienced observer, said that if the Gannet attempted to take flight without as yet having disgorged whatever food it was taking back to its nest the skua would immediately be upon it again.

One would have supposed the skua to be no match for the Gannet, which, in addition to being a bigger bird, is formidably armed. Its body, excluding head and tail, is as long as the overall length of the skua, head and tail included (23 inches). Above all, the Gannet has a massive and pointed bill, a dangerous striking weapon twice as long as the skua's. The skua attacking the Gannet is, perhaps, like a guttersnipe attacking a dandy: he wins by sheer toughness.

On many of the more sparsely inhabited islands, around the precipitous rims of which the cliff-nesting seabirds have their colonies, the interior moorlands and peat bogs belong to the Great Skuas and Arctic Skuas, which have their colonies adjacent to each other. Both species lay their eggs on the open ground. These nesting sites are scattered rather loosely over considerable areas, perhaps over the preponderance of the interior in some of the islands.

The day after we saw the skua attack the Gannet we were on the island of Noss, where I allowed myself to become separated from the rest of the party to explore some cliffs. I had in mind returning directly across the middle of the island to meet the ferry (a rowboat) that was to pick us up at an hour agreed upon in advance. When I finally started inland, across moors where the Great Skuas circled and flapped, or stood on the ground in couples, I suddenly found myself under attack.

To be attacked by a Great Skua is memorable. The bird charges steeply down from a height, wings beating, on a straight trajectory aimed at the center of one's body, only to swerve up at the final instant, clearing one's scalp with a sudden sound of rushing air: *whoosh*. It is like having a railway-train come toward one full tilt—to swerve and roar past in a near miss.

The reaction is panic, especially when two skuas attack successively from different directions, so that one may not see one coming until it is too late to duck. I had already examined the sharp claws of a skua found dead on the moors, and my recollection of what I had read about the ways of the species was that it did not always refrain from striking.

At each of the first few attacks I dropped down prone on my face, hearing the attacker clear my back by inches. Then I started to run toward the shore, the way I had come; but this appeared to incite the birds to redoubled attacks and left me less able to see them coming. Next I found that, by swinging my binoculars over my head at the last minute, I could make the attacker swerve away—but this meant that I had to see it before it arrived. At last, after an intensely busy time, I found that by simply holding my camera-tripod vertically over my head I could ward off the attacks, for the birds were forced to pass that much higher. So I was able to return on time to the ferry-landing unscathed.

While the Great Skua, as one ordinarily sees it at sea, appears to be a lumbering bird, representing power without grace, the Arctic Skua represents grace and power combined. I have never seen its equal for beauty of flight. The size of a Peregrine Falcon, it has the same kind of angled wings, somewhat narrower, but still broader and more powerful than those of Kittiwake or tern. Like the Peregrine, in addition to using its wings for power flight, it is capable of holding them extended (minimizing their angularity) for soaring flight.

It seems to me evident that the three small skuas (the Pomarine, the Arctic, and the Long-tailed) are more closely related to one another than to the Great Skua (formerly put in a separate genus), and that the Great

Skua is closer to the common ancestral form, therefore more primitive. The three are not easy to tell apart in the field. Like our Screech Owl, they are dimorphic, having light and dark forms (also some intermediate forms), although the dark form of the Long-tailed is rare. In all three the two central tail-feathers project beyond the end of the tail, more-or-less as streamers. All three have black caps, are dark bodied but paler underneath, almost white in the light forms. All three, like their bigger relative, have white flashes in their wings.

However much the three differ from the Great Skua in their adult plumages, they are like it in their immature plumages, and the adult plumage of the Great Skua, in turn, is hardly different from its immature plumage. This is the basis for my supposition that the Great Skua best represents the ancestral form of all four, because the principle that the development of the individual tends to recapitulate the evolution of the species appears to be most conspicuously relevant to the differences between the immature and adult plumages of birds. It is the rule that among related species the immatures are more like one another than are the adults, simply because they wear essentially the plumage that had been worn by the adult of a common ancestor. This is striking in such genera of hawks as *Buteo* and *Accipiter*, and in the typical genus of thrushes, *Turdus*; but it is equally true of the gulls and terns, and is, indeed, universal. The fact that the immatures of the three smaller species of skua resemble so closely, in their plumage, the adult Great Skua, which in turn differs hardly at all from its own immature, suggests that they are more developed, further advanced on the evolutionary scale.

A first impression of Arctic Skuas on their nesting grounds is of an explosive vitality, as if the birds had to engage in constant aerial acrobatics at high speed simply to dissipate an intolerable excess of energy.

Their trajectories are arcs, vertical or horizontal, so that they trace continuous arabesques in their flight, varying the speed and depth of their wing-strokes as they veer and swing this way and that. Each bird comes down repeatedly in long sweeps to graze the surface of the moors, only to continue the sweep upward again. When a bird is attacking another, or a human intruder, it executes a remarkable maneuver at the end of the upswing that is the follow-through of each dive, a maneuver that brings it back upon its course for another attack. At the top of the upswing it shoots on up to the vertical and right over onto its back, thus reversing its trajectory and returning downward toward its target without loss of momentum, albeit upside down, simply concluding with a quick wing-over to right itself again. The whole maneuver is so quick that the human eye can hardly follow it.

In all these activities the Arctic Skuas are crying constantly, their principal cry being a gull-like *kawee.*

Since both species of skua had downy young, which one came upon as one walked across the moors, both were presumably at their most aggressive stage in the defence of their own. The Arctic Skuas, however, were distinctly the more aggressive. Over their nesting colonies they were constantly attacking one another in spectacular maneuvers, striking each other with audible clashes. They would also attack the Great Skuas, not only over their own colonies but once, at least, over a Great Skua colony. I never saw a Great Skua attack one of them, and indeed, fast as it is in straightaway flight, it could not have matched them in speed or agility. The Great Skuas' attacks on human intruders, moreover, were not usually as fierce as the one I have described, but the fierceness of the attacks by the Arctic Skuas was always unbridled. Members of our party suffered several strikes on the head by the wings of attacking Arctic Skuas, including one that was felt for hours after.

In addition to attacking the intruder in their nesting colonies, the Arctic Skuas frequently landed on the ground before him, running and stumbling about with waving wings to attract his attention away from a chick that was presumably trying to make itself invisible somewhere in the low ground-cover. (Although this "broken-wing trick," as it is called, is a common practice of ground-nesting birds, I never saw a Great Skua perform it.) On the ground the Arctic Skua, with wings uplifted, looks like a heraldic falcon, its head small but held high, its long hooked bill elegant and fierce.

Individuals doing the "broken-wing trick," by appearing to be in difficulties, often tempted others of their kind to dive on them in attack, and this put them in what was visibly a complicated quandary.

It is worth noting that, without exception, whenever any of us actually came upon a chick of either species, all attacks and efforts to distract us stopped. At that point, when they had failed to prevent our finding the chick, it was as if the parent birds gave up.

In Colgrave Sound, between the islands of Yell and Fetlar, murres, Puffins, and Arctic Terns were flying in two streams, an outward-bound stream of unladen birds, and a returning stream of birds carrying fish back to their nesting sites on the island of Unst. Several Arctic Skuas, like feudal lords with their castles in passes traversed by important routes, were on hand to attack the returning birds. When a tern was attacked it would dodge frantically, the attacker matching its every move, but might at last be forced to drop the fish it was carrying or let the skua pluck it from its bill. At other times persistence would be rewarded: the attacker would veer away, presumably because the prize was not worth so much trouble. When a skua came sweeping in a long curving power-dive toward a Puffin that held a fish crosswise in its bill, the Puffin landed on the water and immediately flipped itself underneath in a surface-dive. The skua, thus foiled, flew off and, a moment later, the Puffin emerged, still with its fish, to resume its flight. On another occasion a Kittiwake engaged in some spectacular dodging, when attacked by an Arctic Skua, but ended by dropping the fish it was carrying, which the skua caught in the air. Often one saw two skuas cooperating in an attack. I don't know whether this ever resulted in a problem of how to divide the booty, as has sometimes been the case among human pirates.

Arctic Skuas often seem to attack other birds capriciously, usually without persisting long in the attack. This behavior may represent a kind of play that keeps them in form and contributes to the dissipation of excess energy, or it may have a more immediately practical purpose when it transpires that the individual attacked has some weakness which makes it an easy prey. Oystercatchers abound everywhere in Shetland, and I recall how one of several skuas flying across the moors turned away on suddenly swift wings to attack one that, quite unable to outspeed it, dodged about desperately with the skua virtually in contact with it, until after a minute the skua flew off to rejoin its traveling companions.

That even the swiftest birds have reason to take these attacks seriously was demonstrated to me more than once. The Rock Dove, which is the wild ancestral form of our domestic pigeon, is a bird of racing flight. On the island of Foula two came flying out of a sea-cave where they were undoubtedly nesting and started across the moors at high speed, when an Arctic Skua cruising nearby took off in chase of one of them. The bird being chased immediately turned and flew back into the cave, emerging for a second time a minute later, when the skua was gone, to follow its companion. A few days later, at Sumburgh Airodrome, I saw why such prudence was advisable. A pigeon, this one the feral variety of the Rock Dove, was flying past when an Arctic Skua sped after and quickly overtook it. In the sport that followed, the skua would strike the fleeing bird and then deliberately let it get away to some distance, whereupon it would overtake it again with the greatest ease and again strike it. Once, when struck, the pigeon tumbled some twenty feet before it recovered its wings and was able to resume its flight. I don't know what would have saved it from being killed if its attacker, having had enough of the sport, had not dropped the attack and made off in time. I suspect that able-bodied Arctic Skuas in Shetland never go hungry, and that they do not need to take the trouble of killing, for food, pigeons that in any case must be more trouble to eat than fish.

The high latitudes of northern and southern hemisphere provide similar habitats separated from each other by half a world. Although on land it is the warm intervening latitudes that have the greatest abundance and luxuriance of life—one thinks of the contrast between a tropical rain-forest and the barren landscapes of the high latitudes—on sea the opposite is the case. The cold oceans of high latitudes swarm with plankton, consequently with fish and seabirds that live on it directly or indirectly. By contrast with the busy traffic of birds everywhere over far northern and far southern seas, in tropical seas one may voyage from dawn to dusk without seeing even one. It follows that the warm waters of mid-earth constitute a formidable barrier to the spread of oceanic species from one polar zone to the other.

Nevertheless, at some time in the past the Fulmar's forebears made the leap from south to north, the Arctic Tern's from north to south. The respective ancestors of either the Great or the Lesser Black-backed Gull and the Black-headed Gull may also have got over the barrier, their descendents in South America being, respectively, the Dominican Gull and the Patagonian Black-headed Gull.

I return, in conclusion, to the uniqueness of the Great Skua in having two such widely separated breeding populations, one in the antarctic and the other in the arctic. Ten thousand miles intervene between the most southern nesters, on the Antarctic continent, and the most northern on the north coast of Iceland, while the gap between the two breeding ranges is more than six and a half thousand miles.

This uniqueness of the Great Skua, in terms of its double range, is compounded by the fact that it is the only bird known to occur deep in the interior of the Antarctic continent, where there is no other form of life to provide it with nourishment. Robert Falcon Scott's record of one at less than 183 miles from the south pole places it so close to the middle of the continent—seven or eight hundred miles from the nearest open water on a flight that must, at least, have been well over a thousand miles—that one must suppose it to have been traversing the continent from coast to coast. This is a testimony to its hardiness, for the south polar regions are far colder and more inclement than the north polar, yet no life has been found as close to the north pole, with the possible exception of microscopic organisms.

Now, however, that the United States Navy maintains a permanent base right at the south pole, it may be that the Great Skua will be attracted to the southernmost point of the world by the prospective foraging that such a base offers. Murphy reports the theory "that two or three seen by Scott and Wilson in latitude 80° 20' S., more than 300 kilometers [186 miles] from open water, had been attracted this enormous distance by the wind-borne odor of the blood of a sledge dog slain some time before!"

Along the northern margin of the Atlantic this

species is not so widely established as to be independent of man. By the middle of the last century human persecution had caused it almost to disappear from Shetland, and it was unknown as a breeding bird in Orkney. W. H. Hudson wrote in his *British Birds* (1895) that the Shetland birds had been reduced to a few pairs, and that it was "scarcely to be hoped that this insignificant remnant will continue to exist many years, when we consider that the childish and contemptible craze of eggshell-collecting is very common. . . ." A change in human habits, however, has since caused it to become common in Shetland and to spread to Orkney.

On the other hand, the Great Skuas that nest all around the edge of the Antarctic continent never, except at isolated points and occasionally, see man on their breeding grounds. For them, man counts for even less than he does for the Storm Petrels. It is on the penguins, rather, that these skuas are dependent, because they live and feed their young, during the breeding season, largely or almost entirely on the eggs and young of the penguins, at the edges of whose nesting colonies, consequently, they establish their own breeding grounds.

And what are penguins?

Penguins belong exclusively to the southern hemisphere and, being flightless, none has ever got across the barrier of equatorial waters into the north temperate and arctic zones. Nevertheless, if only by semantic confusion, penguins were originally birds of the north, and the first penguin identified as such was known in Shetland before the Vikings came there, presumably in the days when an unknown people built the Broch of Mousa. How the penguin, from being a bird of cold northern waters only, became a bird of cold southern waters only, is what we shall see at the outset of the next chapter.

Neither in the first
instance, when man came to them,
nor in the second instance, when they came
to man, were they able to recognize him. —ANONYMOUS

V. THE GREAT AUK, THE LITTLE AUK,
AND MAN

AMONG the seabirds known to sailors from early times
was a large flightless species that bred on desert islands
in the North Atlantic. The members of this species did
not look like birds at all since, in their companies
along the shore, they stood upright like men, wearing
black coats and displaying white shirt-fronts. They had
what seemed more like flippers than wings, which they
used as such when, entering the water, they sub-
merged to swim in the depths like seals. The name by
which the sailors came to identify them was "penguin."

When the sailors saw birds of the same description
in the high latitudes of the southern hemisphere it was
natural that they should call them penguins too. But
the birds that stood upright in their frock coats on the
shores of the southern oceans were not at all related
to the North Atlantic species. The resemblance was

simply the consequence of convergent evolution: unrelated species, adapting themselves in the course of
evolution to the same conditions of life, had made the
same adaptations, and so had come to resemble each
other.

The mariners of centuries past, who attached the
name "penguin" to what we now call the Greak Auk,
shared the traditional assumption that the birds and
beasts of the earth had been created by a benevolent
Providence to minister to man's needs. Moreover, it
occurred to virtually no one that nature, still dominant
over so much of the world, could be as vulnerable to
man's exploitation as it has proved to be. The learned
narrator in Jules Verne's *Twenty Thousand Leagues
under the Sea*, published in 1869, stated what was
simply a truism of the day when he remarked that
"nature's creative power is far beyond man's instinct of
destruction." Presumably the mariners assumed this
too. Since there was food, bait, oil, and feathers to be
had from the Great Auks, which were quite defenceless
on land, they had no compunctions about visiting the
nesting colonies to stock their ships with them, herding the bewildered birds on board across gangplanks.
Then, when the penguin of the north began to be a
rare bird, a competition developed among collectors
to obtain eggs and specimens for the collections they
kept in glass cases. Expeditions were organized for the
purpose of supplying professional dealers who, in turn,
supplied the museums of Europe and America. The
last of the Great Auks was killed in 1844. So, after
some seventy million years of evolution, the species
was extinguished.

There is a finality in the death of a species that there
is not in the death of an individual, for the individual
was bound to die and be replaced anyway. The species
was not bound to die and, once dead, can never be
replaced.

The flightlessness of the Great Auk was peculiar to

it alone among the species of the family *Alcidae* to which it belonged. Of the twenty-two remaining and surviving species all are capable of flight, and all are of very small to moderate size. The deceptive resemblance to penguins exists more-or-less in most of them, but the order of the penguins (*Sphenisciformes*) is one of the most primitive, while the alcids are generally included, today, in the relatively advanced order *Charadriiformes*, which embraces the gulls, terns, skuas, and shorebirds as well.

No one would think to include them in this order on the basis of their outward appearance alone. Although not flightless, they are poor flyers, their wings having become adapted, only less completely than those of the Great Auk, to underwater flying—that is, to the same use as a seal's flippers. Consequently, they can fly through the air only by beating their wings in a rapid mechanical fashion. Aerial flight for them must generally be a matter of local trips rather than long-distance travel, which usually takes place on or under the water.

Although the alcids are all birds of the open seas, they tend to range along the coasts, confining themselves to the continental shelves or to the vicinity of the pack-ice farther north. I suppose they do not face the same danger as the Kittiwakes of being blown inland by persistent gales since, unlike the Kittiwakes, they do not have to hunt their living on the wing. I shall have occasion, however, to mention an exception further on.

Just as the penguins, being swimmers rather than flyers, have never found their way across the barrier of warm water into the northern hemisphere, so the alcids, being swimmers more than flyers, have never found their way into the southern hemisphere. Most of the species, moreover, occur in the high Pacific rather than the high Atlantic.

The seas north of the Scottish mainland abound in alcids. From the steamer going to Shetland one sees them on all sides, their flotillas riding the tossing waves. The ship may pass so close as to lift them with its bow-wave, but leave them undisturbed. More often they either dive at its close approach or skitter over the waves to put down and dive farther on. The commonest are the Common Murres, and this is to be expected, for they nest like the Kittiwakes (and with the Kittiwakes) in dense colonies on the cliffs. The Atlantic Puffins, which nest colonially in burrows on steep seaside slopes or bluffs, are almost as common. Razorbilled Auks one sees less frequently, and Black Guillemots chiefly in sheltered bays and harbors as one comes in to land. These are all the species that occur in the Atlantic except for two: Brünnich's Murre, which breeds far to the north and west of Shetland, and the Dovekie or Little Auk, which breeds way up north.

The Razorbill, a congener of the extinct Great Auk, is essentially a half-size version of it (sixteen as against thirty inches) that has not lost the power of flight. It wears the same suit of black and white, has the same high bill laterally compressed and marked by vertical white stripes against a black background, has the same habit of sitting on land upright, braced by feet that

extend horizontally forward with the full length of the tarsi on the ground. Its nests are hidden in clefts and cavities among the tumbled rocks that pile up at the base of bluffs or cliffs. On such rocks, where they rise to some kind of crest, one sees them perched in small companies, generally with Shags, which nest in similar sites, and a few murres. Individuals or little groups are frequently in flight along the cliffs, like virtually every other species of seabird in the islands.

The Black Guillemot is the most dapper of the alcids, velvety black in its breeding plumage, except for a large white patch on each wing, and with coral-red feet. We found it most often in groups of from two to a dozen in the sheltered waters of narrow inlets bounded by high cliff walls, sometimes swimming about with tails cocked up like those of rails, or perched singly or in pairs on ledges halfway up the walls of such inlets.

The Black Guillemots, in their sartorial elegance, apparently have less taste than the other alcids for being wind-blown in the open sea.

The murres, wearing essentially the same black-and-white costume as the Razorbills, were spectacular by the immense numbers in which they crowded the ledges of their nesting cliffs. At times, like penguins, they looked so human as to appear comical in their solemnity. On horizontal ledges not quite so narrow as those pre-empted by the neighboring Kittiwakes, they stood vertically in rows facing inward, with nothing but rock wall to look at, their backs to the sea and the sky as if disdainful of the immense view. On deep ledges sloping toward the sea they stood in serried row after row, also facing inward; and then one was reminded either of soldiers standing in close formation or of the strap-hangers packed into a New York subway at the rush hour. This kind of crowding requires a high degree of mutual tolerance, for among the Kittiwakes and murres alike incoming birds would sometimes have to land on top of those who had already found a foothold in the crowd, and then struggle to make an opening for themselves; but this appeared never to provoke bad temper.

So far, in these observations, I have stressed the beauty, the grace, and the power of the wide-ranging seabirds that come to Shetland to nest. None of these attributes apply conspicuously to the alcids—except that the murres and especially the Black Guillemots, when they hold their heads high, whether on land or water, present an appearance of elegance. The Puffin does not have even this dignity. Because the initial impression it makes on every observer is comical, it is often referred to in the literature as the clown of seabirds. However, if that is what it is, then it must be regarded as a sad clown.

It is the smallest of the alcids that nest in Shetland, and differs from the others in that, rather than habitually shuffling about on its tarsi, it stands erect on vermilion feet and walks about like, say, a merganser, maintaining a quasi-vertical posture when it is not squatting down to rest. Its basic costume is the typical black and white of the alcids, but what holds one's attention is the round head, the large white disc of its face, the great gaudy bill like some multicolored ceramic clamped onto the face. Of course this is comical; but in the middle of the face, as seen from one side, the gray eye is somehow squeezed between what appear to be two folds of flesh, and the expression this gives it is that of some inner unhappiness. Herein lies the Puffin's dignity. It looks like an unhappy old harlequin, not comical after all.

Although found everywhere, the Puffins were best seen about the cliffs and high bluffs of Sumburgh Head, the southern tip of Shetland proper, where a lighthouse sends its signal out to boats and birds arriving from Fair Isle and Orkney. A precipitous grassy bluff is densely sprinkled with bright flowers and perforated by what might be rabbit burrows; but in front of each burrow one or two Puffins stand among the flowers like aged householders taking the sun on their door-steps.

Puffins have little fear of man, so that, where two or three are resting on an accessible rock, one can approach almost close enough to touch them, and remain there looking them in the eye—man and bird each looking the other in the eye. Only when one approaches still closer, to where one might pick them up, do they rise on their feet at last, sad and reluctant, to drop off into space on whirring wings.

The wings of Puffins seem ridiculously inadequate, mere feathered flippers that they can open up and stick out on either side of their stout bodies. Ordinarily these beaters function like some whirring mechanical device to sustain the bird in flight. Yet one of the most spectacular demonstrations of aerial control I have seen was the performance of Puffins in a high wind at Sumburgh Head. I was lying prone on my stomach at the brink of cliffs that deflected upward a gale from the open sea, so that Fulmars and other birds patrolling

the cliffs were in repeated danger of being blown aloft as by an explosion. The Puffins, facing out to sea, were suspended on this updraft with webbed feet as well as wings spread to it, drifting slightly from side to side, forward and back again, up a bit and sinking down again, like so many Japanese kites at the ends of their strings. Several times one would drift to within four feet of my face. They let the wind carry them backwards as well as forwards, and because they were already so close to the cliffs they were constantly turning their big heads to one side or the other to see what was behind them. They appeared to control their positions perfectly by slight adjustments of wings and feet. When wing-motion was needed the wings merely quivered.

Puffins are partial exceptions to the rule that the alcids confine their wanderings to the coastal shelves. The British *Handbook* reports that they are "not infrequently seen in deep water, several hundred miles from land," and two birds banded in Scotland were recovered in Newfoundland.

As with so many seabirds, at a certain stage the juveniles (one to a nest) are abandoned by their parents to live on their fat, until a night comes when, being sufficiently developed, they emerge from their burrows into the great world, to fall fluttering down into the waiting sea. Each individual thus repeats, entirely on its own impulse, the pioneering of its ancestors for millions of generations past.

Earlier I remarked that the alcids, swimmers more than flyers, are not subject to being blown inland by long-continued winds. The Little Auk or Dovekie, no bigger than a Starling, is an exception, apparently because it lives on plankton at the surface of the sea rather than on fish caught in its depths. In persistent storms that churn the waters, it is probable that this plankton becomes scarce or unavailable at the surface, and then the hungry birds, driven to find food elsewhere, take to the air in congregations of thousands. A Canadian Press dispatch from Ottawa, dated December 21, 1932, reports that: "Flocks of the Arctic sea birds have been observed passing high above Quebec toward Montreal, Ottawa and Toronto. In a few days they will be found dead in inland waters. No one knows what causes the death flight."

I have at hand a newspaper clipping of November 22, 1932 reporting how, the previous day, Dovekies had rained on New York City, falling exhausted into the streets of Manhattan to be picked up by passers-by on the pavements. ("Most of the finders," the *New York Herald Tribune* reported, "believed they had baby penguins.")

The habitat of this Little Auk is arctic seas in which, night and day, the combers in endless procession wash from horizon to horizon, everywhere breaking into whitecaps with a little sigh. That of the human passers-by consists of cement pavements from which doors

Common Murres

open into chambers with electric light and warmth; it consists of restaurants and movie-theaters; it consists of salons where intellectuals, cocktail-glasses in hand, explain the nature of the world in whatever terms represent the fashion of the day. Auk and man alike belong to the category of life-on-earth, they belong to what is one world. But the vision of neither is broad enough to comprehend what the other represents. For the man under the street-lights, hurrying home from his office, the city is the only reality. He does not know what to make of the little creature that has fallen out of the open sky; and the little creature looks with blank eyes at the narrow streets where the hordes of pedestrians trample the pavements.

How, in this one world of auks and men, shall we ever establish the correspondence between them?

The playful phalaropes, always awake,
Dancing like midges in the slow whale's wake. —ANONYMOUS

VI. SEAGOING SANDPIPERS

AND SOME RELATIVES

EVERYONE who knows birds has a special place in his heart for the shorebirds. They represent the ultimate refinement of living forms, together with the ultimate intensity of life. In season, coastal beaches the world over are alive with them. Sometimes they cover the sand like a moving carpet—say of Sanderlings all running together on whirring feet that are surely activated by watchworks. Suddenly the carpet is lifted as by a puff of wind, transformed now into a swarm that moves like one being, that darts along the trough of the wave, that slips in between successive breakers, now seen, now hidden.

When we think of the shorebirds we think not only of sandpipers but also of plovers, more strikingly marked, more thinly distributed than Sanderlings over the beaches and also over the tumbled rocks against which the surf breaks.

Finally, not the least distinction of shorebirds: many have cries that, uttered in two or three syllables as they take flight, are the most musical sounds in nature. I know of no other sound that equals them in purity except the song of the Brown-backed Solitaire of Central America.

Is it not strange, when we know these birds only as they outwardly show themselves, that the Sanderling, the Great Auk, and the skua of the antarctic should be associated as members of one order, the *Charadriiformes*?

In numbers the shorebirds dominate the order. They count 314 species, to twenty-two for the alcids, to eighty-nine for gulls, terns, and skuas. These 314 themselves represent a wide range of variety, including species that we hardly think of as shorebirds at all: the jaçanas of lily-ponds in tropical rain-forest, looking like aberrant gallinules; the lapwings flapping along on broad, rounded wings; the pratincoles, in flight and appearance between the terns and the swallows; the seedsnipe of South American barrens, looking not unlike finches; the tall and elegant avocets; the piratical sheathbills of the southern hemisphere, which avoid water and are reported by Murphy to have "the general appearance, gait, and flight of a pigeon, with the beak and voice of a crow." Nor are seedsnipe and sheathbills the only members of the group for which either "shorebird" or "wader" (the British term) is a misnomer. There are the woodcocks, the snipe, the Upland Sandpiper, the Killdeer, the stone curlews, the coursers, and other species of forest, field, or desert.

We would have to report to any man from Mars that a feature of life on our planet is its variety.

No one who sees a phalarope on land can have any hesitation in classing it with the shorebirds, and if he does not already know that it is a phalarope he must suppose it to be one of the smaller sandpipers. It is, in fact, a member of the sandpiper family.

The first phalarope I ever saw, and the only one before my visit to Shetland, was from shipboard in mid-Atlantic. On a calm sunny day, looking out over a sea that was otherwise empty, I caught sight of what was surely a small sandpiper in darting flight over the slowly heaving surface. My first reaction was incredulity to see a bird of the beaches so far from land—when suddenly it had stopped and was sitting on the great ocean itself, slowly lifted and lowered by the swell, head high, turning about this way and that, bobbing as it swam, making darting movements with its bill. Only then did I know it for a phalarope.

Against the luminous sea such a speck showed only as a silhouette, color and markings indiscernible. There was no telling which of the world's three species of phalarope it was—probably either a Gray or a Red-necked Phalarope so far east in the Atlantic. Both are completely pelagic. Except in the brief breeding season they normally live their lives out of sight of land in the open oceans, no matter what the weather. The question arises how they survive the tempests at sea when, under the fury of the wind, the waves lash the sky day after day and all night long.

> Poor naked wretches wheresoe'er you are,
> That bide the pelting of this pitiless storm. . . .

Whalers used to take a particular interest in these seagoing sandpipers, for they followed whales swimming below the surface in order to land on them, when they came above it, and run about on their backs in search of parasites. (Few are the whales left them today!)

All three species of phalarope nest high in the northern hemisphere but winter down to the latitudes of South Africa and the Falkland Islands. They differ from typical sandpipers by lobes on their toes and dense underplumage for swimming. Another distinction is in the bright colors of their breeding plumage. Finally, small as they are, they have an elongated elegance of form such as one finds only in the most slender of the sandpipers, which are generally much taller. Their round heads are carried high on necks like stems, and in the species I am about to deal with the bills are like needles.

An unexplained peculiarity of the phalaropes is that the roles of the sexes are reversed in all except what is unalterable, the act of mating and the laying of eggs. The female is larger and more brightly colored. She aggressively courts the male, who may be coy, and she attacks other females. He is the one who builds the nest, incubates the eggs she has laid, broods, feeds, and cares for the young—while she, abandoning the whole business at an early stage, goes off with her female cronies to enjoy an irresponsible life offshore. What the reason is for this reversal of roles invites inquiry and speculation.

The Red-necked Phalarope was almost extirpated in Shetland during the nineteenth and early twentieth centuries by those who collected for display in glass cases the eggs and mounted specimens of rare species —eggs and specimens that increased in value as collecting made the species rarer, until the ultimate value was achieved by their extinction. Fortunately, this method of genocide has drastically diminished as it has, at last, taken on the aspect of a public scandal rather than a respectable occupation of those interested in natural history. So old threats to the survival of species pass while new ones (e.g. the pesticides) arise. For some twenty years now, the population of breeding phalaropes in Shetland has, according to the estimates, remained at about thirty pairs. This makes it the rarest of any species breeding in the islands that I shall have occasion to discuss in these observations.

The fresh-water Loch of Spiggie, a mile and a half long, is roughly oval in shape. At one of its narrow ends it is separated from the open ocean by the length of an oceanic inlet and a strip of land, like a dike, some three hundred feet wide. Kittiwakes come and go in continuous streams across this dike, the loch being one of many such places that they visit to bathe and regale themselves. Other gulls, terns, skuas, Mallards, and Moorhens move on or over its surface, or through the fringing reeds. At one point its shoreline becomes highly irregular, with fingers or pockets of shallow water half clothed in broad-leaved water plants. A pair of Red-necked Phalaropes that had presumably started

a nest here were conspicuously in evidence, small as
they were, because their restless vitality kept them
constantly in a state of such active movement, whether
on land, on the water, or in the air. The difficulty in
observing them was not that of getting close enough,
for they would repeatedly land on the water within
twenty or thirty feet of the observer. But they did not
stay. They flitted off again in darting flight over the
grasses, down again and hidden from view, now up
again, repeatedly uttering a single note, a *twit*, often
excitedly and in rapid succession. Nothing could exceed
their delicacy and elegance when on the water or on
land. Obviously they were the aristocrats of some
Lilliputian kingdom. On land they ran about with an
agility one would not have expected in birds that, for
three-quarters of every year, hardly have occasion to
touch anything solid with their feet. On the water they

rode high, their little heads on stalks, turning about
this way and that, repeatedly touching the surface on
one side or another with the needle tips of their bills.
Both wore a pattern of gray and white (bolder in the
female) and both had an orange-red stain (brighter
and more extensive in the female) that ran down from
the back of the head over the throat, making each look
like some flower of the marsh-weed through which it
swam.

No Venetian ever blew anything as delicate in glass.
No photograph can do justice to it; no painter ever has.
One needs the vast setting of sky and water to see how
small the bird is. The daintiness of its hesitating and
darting flight could never be reproduced.

Oystercatchers are shorebirds too, but quite different
from phalaropes. Heavy-bodied, the size of crows, and
as noisy as Herring Gulls, they occur in temperate and
tropical zones all around the world, from as far north
as Iceland to as far south as New Zealand. Their
several geographical forms are so much alike that the
taxonomists remain at a loss to know whether they
should be considered all one species or any number up
to six.

I, myself, had seen Oystercatchers only occasionally, in pairs or little flocks on the east coast of the
United States, or as scattered individuals of the melan-
istic form (all-black plumage) on the Oregon coast.
This did not prepare me for their overwhelming presence in Scotland and Shetland.

When Dr. Austin wrote that "nowhere are oystercatchers abundant," he was overlooking the northern
half of Britain. James Fisher estimates that the breeding population of the British Isles is between twenty
and forty thousand pairs, most of which must, I judge,
be in the north. It has been on the increase in Britain.
Although primarily a coastal bird, it has now spread

as a breeding bird over the interior moorlands of north England and Scotland, even to as high as 1,800 feet in the highlands.

Certainly I was not prepared for what I saw from the train window soon after leaving Edinburgh for Aberdeen. All along, in fields and meadows as well as by the shores of ocean and stream, individuals, pairs, or little companies of Oystercatchers were standing about or flying. In Shetland they were everywhere, inland as on the coasts, conspicuous by their striking appearance and vociferous boldness. Their colors and markings, no less than their cries, seemed designed to call attention to themselves.

Male and female wear the same harlequin costume. They are black and white in big patches, with pink feet, and with long orange-red bills in the shape of chisels, laterally compressed, which they use to force mussel shells apart and pry limpets off rocks. The bills are constantly opening like scissors as the birds cry aloud. Now that they have spread inland and upland they have also taken to following the plow in flocks, like some of the inland gulls, using their great colored bills to pick up insects that it has uncovered.

Wherever one walks in Shetland several are likely to be circling overhead with shallow wing-beats, apparently objecting to one's presence, crying *klee-eep klee-eep* to pierce one's ears, or uttering other notes including, occasionally, piping, bubbling, trilling sounds.

My intention in these observations is to comment merely on what I found remarkable in the bird-life of Shetland. I therefore omit, for the most part, what is no different in Shetland from what we are familiar with farther south. There were, for example, a variety of shorebirds—Common Sandpipers, Dunlin, Redshanks, Turnstones, Ringed Plovers, Lapwings—but because they appeared in Shetland as they appear elsewhere I shall not discuss them.

I have the impression, however, that as one moves up from the tropics toward the arctic a certain simplification and clarification manifests itself in the avifauna as a whole and in the status of particular species. The ecology becomes less complicated than in the tropics, where innumerable kinds of birds are so mixed up together that an observer could spend a lifetime trying to get a complete picture of even an area limited to a few square miles, and of the place that each species occupied in it, without succeeding. In northern lands beyond tree-line, like Shetland, there are far fewer species, but those there are live lives open to the view, and many are likely to be found in such concentrations as are never seen in warm countries. (Since this is partly a matter of the vegetative setting, an exception would have to be made if, for example, one were comparing a Scandinavian spruce forest with the Sahara Desert; but this would be to strain for exceptions.) The Oystercatcher illustrates my generalization; it is widely distributed in warm temperate and tropical latitudes, but never in such concentrated abundance as one finds it when one has got far enough north in the British Isles.

The concentrations of birds in the north represent, in part, uniformity of habitat. A bird of treeless rolling country will find patches of such country farther south, but here it is all that. Presumably this explains the conspicuousness of the Curlews, which are to be seen commonly, as individuals or couples, standing on the moors, or circling over them with their long decurved bills opening repeatedly to release, like bells ringing, the sound that gives them their name. (The French name, *Courlis*, is closer to it, especially if one accents the second syllable: *coor-lý*.)

The Curlew is even larger than the Oystercatcher— is, in fact, the largest of European shorebirds, only slightly surpassed in overall length by the similar Long-billed Curlew of North America. It is a brown streaked bird, remarkable for its thin downward-curving bill, like some surgical instrument, which may be half as long as the rest of its body. (I ask myself whether in all the world there are any birds except the toucans that have longer bills in proportion to their bodies.)

The Curlew is at the southern limit of its breeding-range around Geneva, where I live. At the northern limit, in Shetland and along the Norwegian coast, it overlaps the breeding range of its smaller and more northerly congener, the Whimbrel. Whimbrels were fewer than Curlews in Shetland, but there were enough of them so that one had to be careful, in identification, to distinguish the one species from the other.

The Snipe, like the Oystercatcher, is cosmopolitan. It breeds on the ground in wet meadows throughout most of the north temperate zone above the warmer latitudes (above the Mediterranean and the American South), throughout the south temperate zone (except Australia and New Zealand), and over a large part of both the American and the African tropics—as far north as Iceland, as far south as Tierra del Fuego, and even in parts of South America dominated by tropical rain-forest.

Unlike the Oystercatcher, but like its own close relatives the woodcocks, it is a bird of cryptic habit. A small, protectively colored bird, mottled or streaked with brown, it conceals itself so well in the dense grass of its habitat that passersby ordinarily learn of its presence only when, accidentally, they come close enough to flush it. Then, as if catapulted, it shoots into the sky on a zigzag trajectory, repeatedly uttering a harsh single note. It is almost as abrupt in returning to earth, dropping vertically into the grass like a spent rocket.

Seen in flight, or on the rare occasions when one may happen to find it feeding on an open mudbank, it is remarkable for the disproportion between its long straight bill and the little body that carries it. Perched or flying, it carries this bill pointed downward, as if resting on its breast, and although in measurable terms it is not quite as disproportionate as the Curlew's scimitar, it makes the bird seem more of a freak.

My reason for including the Snipe in this account is that I found the cryptic creature so much less cryptic in Shetland than anywhere else I had seen it, whether in Europe or America. Again, as in the case of Oyster-catcher and Curlew, a species that occurs so far north is relatively abundant and, in so open a setting, observable.

The Snipe's relative abundance was attested by the frequency with which we observed it in its courtship flight—which would, after all, attract attention to it equally wherever it was performed. The male circles high over its breeding ground on rapidly beating wings, repeatedly diving and recovering in a U-curve that carries it up again to its pitch. At the bottom of each dive one hears a soft booming sound, like wind in a barrel but with an extreme vibrato. (The sound is produced during the dive itself, by outer tail-feathers spread wide to the wind, but is likely to reach the observer only when the bird has reached bottom and is turning up again.)

The Snipe's abundance is not in itself surprising, for most of the surface of the islands is Snipe habitat. Even the tops of the moorland hills are likely to be squishy with moisture underfoot, and a large part of the surface is peat bog. Add to this that in Scotland and the surrounding islands the Snipe is less restricted in its habitat than elsewhere, frequently making itself at home in the heather of dry upland hills.

As one drives along the narrow roads of Shetland one sometimes sees Snipe standing in the open fields on either side, as one sees Curlews. What is even more surprising is to see them perched on roadside fence-posts (like Meadowlarks in the American West), not taking off even when one's car passes within a few feet, reluctant to take off even when the car stops. There is something peculiarly moving in the experience of having a creature known as the shyest of the shy unexpectedly accept the human presence without fear. Suddenly one feels that the millennium, when the lion and the lamb shall lie down together, is at hand.

No less than the reader of these notes, phalarope and Snipe, Curlew and Oystercatcher represent life on earth. One cannot even be sure that they are less important in whatever may be the great scheme of things.

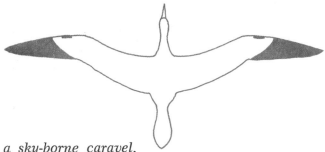

The gannet, like a sky-borne caravel,

Coursing the sunlit seas with sails full spread. —FROM THE PORTUGUES

VII. THE GANNET AND THE

ANCIENT SHAG

THERE are many species of birds that, because they pass their lives in an environment of salt water, are properly called seabirds. Of the twenty-seven avian orders in the world, however, only two are composed exclusively of such species: the penguins (*Sphenisciformes*) and the albatross-petrel order (*Procellariiformes*). The order *Pelecaniformes* is also composed exclusively of water birds, but many of them are fresh-water sailors.

The *Pelecaniformes* are distinguished from other birds in that all four toes are connected by webs, the hind one being pulled around for the purpose. They are also unique among seabirds in being altricial rather than praecocial. That is, like our familiar garden birds, the young hatch when they are still only embryonic dabs of flesh, rather than waiting like ducklings until, already covered with down, they can run about and swim. Merely as a matter of speculation, I am tempted to associate this altricial habit with the fact that their order belongs predominantly to the warmer parts of the earth. Altricial birds undergo, outside the egg, a development that praecocial birds undergo inside it, and perhaps there is less reason why it should not take place outside where the total transition from germ to fully fledged bird does not have to be fitted into a short and relatively cold summer. The penalty of being a praecocial bird is that one has to lay such a large egg, and birds of low latitudes may have less need to pay it.

In the Caribbean area, where I formerly lived and traveled, the majority of the birds one sees over the ocean are *Pelecaniformes*: pelicans, boobies, frigate birds, and tropic-birds. On inland waters one sees cormorants and anhingas, which are also members of the order. It follows that, when I find Gannets and cormorants in high northern latitudes they strike me as belonging to a different world from that of the Storm Petrel, the Fulmar, the skuas, and the alcids; for I think of them as outlying representatives of tropical families, not really belonging to the world of tundra, fog, and cold glaucous seas. When I analyze my feelings, I find that I have hesitated to include in these observations an account of that great seabird, the Gannet, which is one of the prominent cliff-nesters of Shetland, simply because of an unconscious disposition to regard it as not really belonging.

Of some ten species of its family and genus in the world, the Gannet is the only one that ranges outside tropical and subtropical waters. In addition to its North Atlantic population, it has a population that breeds in South Africa and another in Australia and New Zealand; and while the differences between these populations, so widely separated, might allow one to consider them separate species, they are generally regarded today as varieties of one only.

In the New World the Gannet of the North Atlantic nests only about the Gulf of St. Lawrence. Otherwise it nests along an arc extending from Iceland through Faroe and the British Isles to the north coast of

France. First-year birds bred in the Old World migrate as far as the coast of tropical Africa; in their second year they are less disposed to go so far; and by the time they have become fully adult the migratory impulse appears to be lost entirely, so that after the nesting season they simply disperse at random over the ocean. Perhaps this is a manifestation of the principle, mentioned in Chapter IV, that the development of the individual tends to recapitulate the evolution of its kind, the immature birds being atavistically moved, as the adults no longer are, to return to ancestral haunts along ancestral migration-routes.

The Gannet is the largest of the seabirds that nest in the temperate zones of the northern hemisphere, and in its adult plumage the most obviously beautiful. None is more elegantly dressed. Like other large birds of snow-white plumage—Snow Geese, Eiders, storks, the Ghiesbrecht's Hawks of the American tropics, Swallow-tailed Kites, white pelicans, albatrosses—it has black wing-tips. Such a bird should be first seen over a sea that reflects a blue sky with white clouds, when it appears as a flying cross with long tapering limbs. It has a neck somewhat shorter than that of a goose, and a straight bill that tapers to a point. The big bird tapers to a point at the other end too, where the long tail is wedge-shaped. Its wings are narrower in proportion than those of terns, longer and more pointed than those of gulls. Generally the Gannet is to be seen flying at a height above the sea, beating its great wings, gliding, then beating them again. When it spies below it the relatively large fish on which it feeds, it dives like an immense tern, its wings close to its body, closing them completely just before the great splash in which it disappears—to bob up again after an interval.

Where Gannets congregate in flocks over shoals of fish they may be seen in a continuous rain of falling bodies upon the sea, each sending up its splash. Since

I have never, myself, had a good view of this famous spectacle, I can do no better than to quote here Murphy's description of a closely similar species, the Peruvian Booby, of which he writes: "the scene of thousands striking the ocean like hissing hailstones is one that beggars description." But what immense hailstones they are!

The Gannet is said to have been taken in fishermen's nets at a depth of ninety feet, but although it swims downward in pursuit of its prey a doubt about this figure must remain as long as one cannot quite exclude the possibility of individuals becoming entangled in nets being hauled up from such depths.

Seen close up, whether at rest or on the wing, the Gannet shows some finer points of sartorial distinction. Its head and neck are tinged with pale yellow, giving a subtle touch of warmth to the cold plumage, like the pink that tinges the breast of the drake Goosander. The bluish color of the bill extends back to provide a dark setting for the glaring white eye, which appears as if it were set like an agate into the bill itself. The effect is curious. The two agate eyes, set so close together on either side of the bill, give an impression of narrow-minded intensity.

There are just two nesting colonies of Gannets in Shetland: one at its northernmost tip, around Hermaness, the other on the Isle of Noss, which stands in the North Sea at the latitude of Lerwick. They are new colonies, since the one at Noss was begun in 1914, the one at Hermaness in 1917, but they have grown

Isle of Noss

steadily until by 1965 each was estimated to contain between four and five thousand nests. Presumably this does not represent a general expansion of the North Atlantic population but merely a local development.

The six-hundred-foot cliffs at the south end of Noss are one of the great centers for cliff-nesting seabirds in the North Atlantic. They are all there, the alcids, the Kittiwakes, and the Shags, as well as the Gannets. The Kittiwakes that nest here have not suffered from competition for nesting-sites by the expanding colony of Gannets, since Gannets could not use such narrow ledges as are theirs; but the murres have had to give way, although they remain common in their military ranks on the ledges.

The Gannet colony is on one great rock, a sort of Gibraltar, that juts into the sea. (It is the highest point to be seen in the accompanying illustration.)

From a distance what one sees is a blizzard of birds swirling around it, becoming sparser as it extends out toward the open ocean. Close to, one sees that the ledges are packed with bulky nests of seaweed, with adults perched upon them and in continuous movement; and with fat downy young, their white bodies like stuffed wool-sacks. The rock-face and the ledges are heavily whitewashed, and an acrid smell pervades the atmosphere—the same smell, presumably, as hangs over the guano islands off the coast of Peru, where the Peruvian Booby, together with other members of its order, once piled up a wealth that exceeded the gold of the Inca, in the form of guano deposits covering the islands to depths of a hundred and eighty feet or more. (Not the productivity of the Peruvian birds, phenomenal as it is, but the lack of rain accounts for the uniqueness of these accumulations.)

In the midst of the colony, or about its edges, Kittiwakes also nest in rows; and murres; and Fulmars singly; and Shags here and there; and a pair of Ravens are about that may well have their nests here too. As at all such colonies, the din is incessant.

The Gannets resemble many other species of seabirds, perhaps most, in abandoning their young in the nest after first fattening them up so that they can go without food for a month or more. Some ten days after its parents have left their sole offspring of the year, it flutters and falls from its nest to the sea. There, still unable to fly, it is unable to feed itself. The Venables report that the fledglings from Noss "swim slowly S.E. or S.S.E. [in obedience, perhaps, to the atavistic migratory impulse that will later be lost altogether] . . . and are thinly distributed over the sea (less than one per square mile)." After some two to three weeks (just how long is unknown) they are able to fly and therefore to catch fish, at last, by diving from aloft. Then, presumably, they continue on toward Africa.

And below on a rock against the grey sea fretted,
Pipe-necked and stationary and silhouetted,
Cormorants stood in a wise, black, equal row
Above the nests and long blue eggs we know. —J. C. SQUIRE

The cormorants are not without their claims on this wide world, having inhabited it for fifty million years (fifty times as long as we men).

Presumably because they are dark, with an oily sheen to their plumage, they have a sinister reputation in our literature. According to Milton, when Satan first stole into Paradise with the intention of corrupting God's noblest creatures, he flew up

> . . . and on the Tree of Life,
> The middle tree and highest there that grew,
> Sat like a cormorant . . .

(Defeated on his first attempt, on the second he took the guise of a serpent.)

Moreover, the cormorant's notorious appetite has made it a symbol of greed. Its reputation undoubtedly owes much to human fishermen, who have always resented the competition it gives them. (But it was on the fishing-grounds forty-nine million years before they were!) In our tradition, birds were made to serve men, not to rival them. When God created men he said: "Let them have dominion . . . over the birds of the air." A limited dominion of the sort has been established in the Orient, where fishermen use tame cormorants to fish for them from small boats. The birds operate under water on leashes, with leather rings around their necks to prevent swallowing.

All species of cormorant have snaky necks. They swim on the surface with bills pointed upward, bodies sloping down and blending into the water, the bodies so low in the water that sometimes they hardly show at all. Instead of diving from the air like Gannets, they plunge from the surface to pursue fish below. Their style of flight is similar to that of loons and geese. However, one species in the Galápagos Islands, having had no need for its wings over countless millennia, has become flightless, just as the Great Auk did in like circumstances. Now that man has arrived on the scene, however, and is at last assuming dominion over the world, the Flightless Cormorant of the Galápagos faces extinction.

All species of cormorant are tied to land by a disability curious in aquatic birds. Their plumage is not completely waterproof, so that they are constantly having to leave the water to dry it out, perched almost vertically on rock or post, with wings extended to sunlight or breeze. In this position they look heraldic, as Satan must have atop the Tree of Life. Although they swim like loons and ducks and are at home among the fishes in the depths, the fact that their plumage gradually soaks up water prevents them from resting indefinitely on the surface to preen and regale themselves. They have to rest and preen on the rocks or

posts where they also spread their sails to dry. It follows that, although they are mainly marine, they cannot range far from land. Perhaps this fits in with the fact that they tend to be remarkably sedentary, not engaging in long migrations or wanderings. But there must be a reason why, after fifty million years, these water birds are not waterproof; there must be some advantage that outweighs the obvious disadvantage.

The cormorants of the world total about thirty species, only two of which occur in the British Isles. Some of the thirty are called shags, a generic name that sailors have given them; but this does not imply a difference, for shags are cormorants like any others. Because the English vernacular names came into being when the British thought of the birds that occurred in Britain as British birds only, and when the existence of birds elsewhere had no great practical import, their names often do not include adjectives to distinguish the "British" species from others that are not "British." The two British species are called simply the Cormorant and the Shag.

The Cormorant is equally at home on the rocky coast of Britain, where it lives on North Atlantic fish, and far from salt water in the rain-forests of east Africa. It is at home in Siberia and in India. It nests from well above the arctic circle, in Greenland and northernmost Scandinavia, to as far south as the southern tip of New Zealand. Like that other species of the Old World, the Gannet, it also has a North American breeding colony where the St. Lawrence empties into the Atlantic. Farther south along the Atlantic shores of the New World, however, it is replaced by the Double-crested Cormorant.

The smaller Shag is limited to the seashores of Europe, from northern Scandinavia and Iceland down and around to the Black Sea, with a slight extension into Africa across the Straits of Gibraltar. It is exclusively maritime, never going inland. It ranges farther out from shore in its fishing expeditions and hunts in deeper waters than the Cormorant—a more salty bird altogether.

The Cormorant has become far less common in Shetland than it was a century ago, for no reason that I am able to suggest. On two occasions I saw companies of five or six in flight—and that was all. The Shag, on the other hand, is abundant throughout the islands and, if one can judge from the remains found in the middens of Jarlshof, a site of pre-Viking and Viking settlements near Sumburgh Head, its abundance goes back to prehistoric times. Certainly Shetland, so girt and penetrated by the sea, so naked to the elements, suits the Shag better than it does the Cormorant.

The Shag is uniformly dark, its plumage showing a greenish sheen. I can do no better than quote the description of it in Paul Géroudet's *Water-birds with Webbed Feet*, as translated from the French by Phyllis Barclay-Smith. "At the foot of the jagged cliffs of Finisterre, on reefs battered by foam-flecked waves, the Shags stand like bronze statues polished by the spray." Looking down from cliff and bluff on the rugged Shetland shores below, where the surf came in and withdrew incessantly, one saw them posed on the rocks with Razorbills; one saw them on the broader ledges near the bottoms of the cliffs in the company of the other cliff-dwellers, usually on bulky nests just inside the entrances to the thundering sea-caves invaded by the surf. Here at the cavernous portals darkness began, and one was left to surmise, from the traffic of entering and departing birds, the existence of other nests beyond. Indeed, the birds pouring in and out of this darkness, which may have led down into an unimaginable realm, made the Cormorant's association with Satan plausible.

For forty-nine million years there were shags in the world, but no men. Then one of the primates began to distinguish himself from others (while the old shags continued to catch fish and stand spread-eagled on the rocks). After some nine hundred and ninety-five thousand more years the new primate, conscious of his distinction as man, began to make his works conspicuous on the face of the earth. (The shags continued to fish and stand spread-eagled on the rocks.) Something a bit less than five thousand years later, he began to fill all the land surfaces of the earth, to establish his dominion, to transform the planet into a human world. He was not concerned with the future of *being* as such, or with the future of *life* as such, but with the future of himself. He invented forms of philosophy that took account of himself alone, leaving out the Shag, the Storm Petrel, the Fulmar, the skua, the auk, the phalarope, the gull, and the Gannet. They had no credentials that man need honor in what he had now established as his own world.

Among the foreseeable possibilities for the future, one is that man, having arrived only a million years ago, will go on for another forty-nine million, in the course of which he will begin to learn at first hand how big the universe is. He will go fishing in the Milky Way—thinking, perhaps, that it belongs to him. But at the end of those forty-nine million years another creature may arise, and it may refashion the Milky Way to suit itself. Then man, lacking credentials, may come to seem no more important than a Shag.

O let your strong imagination turn
The great wheel backward, until Troy unburn,
And then unbuild, and seven Troys below
Rise out of death, and dwindle, and outflow,
Till all have passed, and none has yet been there:
Back, ever back. Our birds still crossed the air;
Beyond our myriad changing generations
Still built, unchanged, their known inhabitations. –J. C. SQUIRE

VIII. BIRDS OF THE PAST AND BIRDS
OF THE FUTURE

IT IS THOUGHT that loons, which are among the most primitive of birds, have been on earth a hundred million years. One might expect that over so much time their order would have proliferated in many directions, like other orders I have mentioned, producing a wide variety of families, genera, and species. Instead, all we have is one family containing one genus composed of four species. But what a distinctive order it is all the same, its four members so like one another and so unlike any other birds!

Presumably the order originated in the high latitudes of the northern hemisphere, to which the four species are still confined. Although they are swift flyers, known to make overland flights of a thousand miles or more, they have not been among the great explorers. They have remained where they were, not bothering to see what lies south of their home latitudes.

Loons, although they have the smallest wing-area

for their weight of any birds that fly, have the same style of flight as cormorants, but their wings are narrower, their feet extend out where their tails should be, and altogether they look thinner of body and wing, more elongated, more skeletal than other birds of similar flight. They have their own geometry.

Whether on the Atlantic coast of the United States or on the Lake of Geneva, we ordinarily know loons only in the bleak plumage that matches their surroundings in winter, not in the sharply contrasting modernistic patterns that they wear for the breeding season. I have boyhood memories, however, of summer canoe-trips through chains of lakes in the forests of New England where human habitation was, as yet, only' scattered. I remember sleeping in the open one night under evergreens by the shore of a forest lake. I lay there long before I could sleep, listening to the musical wailing of a pair of Common Loons in the darkness out over the water, long wails that rose to chilling climaxes, only to break down in what sounded like laughter. Next morning I saw the two of them on water dark or dappled where it reflected the hemlocks, light where it mirrored the sky. Their two bodies, moving monumentally over its surface, were also dark and dappled, with areas of light.

All that is gone now. Today on those same lakes motorboats race where the loons swam; and where the hemlocks stood the automobiles roar past. The new estivants that have replaced the loons, coming from the cities farther south, frolic in sport clothes of sharply contrasting modernistic patterns, more colorful than those of the loons, filling the air with their own cries and laughter. They represent the achievement of the dominion over the earth and all its creatures that had been promised, in the first chapter of *Genesis*, to the only being that God made in his own image.

Besides the Common Loon of the New England lakes, the other loon we know in the eastern United States is the smaller Red-throated Loon, with its upturned bill. It does not breed south of Canada, so that we see it only in winter, almost always offshore in the Atlantic, a dim silhouette glimpsed in the vapors of the wintry ocean. In Shetland, however, it is a common breeding bird. My impression was that on virtually every fresh-water loch in the bare moorlands there was an adult loon acting as nanny to a well-grown young dressed in chocolate-colored down. Because of the predilection of this species for breeding on such small bodies of water, to which the parent is held by the presence of its flightless young, observation was easy. Only one parent was to be seen at a time, however, for one would be hunting at sea while the other was on duty.

At the approach of the human observers the parent on duty—its shapely head pastel-gray, the solid-red isosceles triangle on its throat Euclidean in its perfec-tion—would sink low in the water until the juncture of back and neck was awash; or it would submerge completely, re-appearing after a few seconds and swimming after its charge. It would manifest its anxi-ety by a few harsh barks.

In the clear dawn on Mousa, after we had watched the Storm Petrels change their guard at an ancient fortress, walking over the moors I found a loch no bigger than a pond, with a half-grown young loon on it. Soon there were five adults circling overhead and barking, the sun lighting them from below. And there were Wrens singing among the tumbled rocks on the nearby shore, Skylarks aloft, Wheatears darting in the heather, Great Skuas circling, Arctic Terns diving, Oystercatchers crying and crying; and Fulmars and gulls, and how much else if one looked about?—while the sea-swells advancing from the east glittered in the light of all creation's new day.

There is one point in the world where loons have entered into arrangements with men. "On the Inland

Sea of Japan near Seto," Dr. Austin writes, "the fishermen depend on Red-throated and Arctic loons to drive the fish into schools so they can be netted easily. These Japanese fishermen take pains to avoid frightening the birds or hurting them in their nets, and the loons have become so tame they swim among the schooling fish right next to the fishing boats."

A similar relationship has been established in Iceland and elsewhere between the Common Eider and man. The female eiders line their nests with eiderdown plucked from their breasts, which is then collected by men for use in feather-bedding. The men not only protect the eiders in return, but encourage them to nest about human communities in special structures set up for the purpose. The eiders, then, become as domestic as House Sparrows in a farmyard.

The whole great family of ducks, geese, and swans, to which the eider belongs, seems to have a native inclination for assuming a domesticated role inside human civilization. Throughout Europe, now, the Mute Swans live a feral, unconfined life, but in dependence on men. One sees them about the clanging dockyards in the Port of Hamburg as well as on the tranquil waters of Geneva (where the cantonal government maintains a special officer to look after their welfare); and everywhere they take food from the hand. In Geneva wild Pochards and Tufted Ducks sleep or feed under bridges over which the traffic roars, only a few feet from pedestrians who look down on them, although outside the city hunters have forced them to cultivate an extreme wariness, to the point where one can hardly approach within half a mile of their flocks. In settlements on the Baltic coast of Sweden, where they are provided with nest-boxes and protected for the sake of their eggs, I have seen those saw-toothed fish-eating ducks, the Goosanders, as tame as barnyard fowl.

Persecution, apparently, cannot make the eider wild. It seems unable to take account of men with shotguns.

Once, in the Öre Sound between Denmark and Sweden, I saw two men row up to within close range of an adult male eider, then take their time to aim and fire. After wounding it sufficiently to catch it alive, they beat it to death with their oars. Every fall a few eiders, generally first-year birds that have gone astray (for their habitat is salt-water), reach the Lake of Geneva. Because they are unsuspicious, allowing a close approach, there are none left by the time the winter is half over. (Now at last, however, waterfowl hunting in the Canton of Geneva is being constantly reduced by legal restrictions that represent the public conscience, and the hunters are becoming constantly fewer, so that the time may be at hand when wintering eiders will survive to return north in the spring.)

Like the Great Skua, the eider is too heavily built to be graceful. Of all our ducks it is the most stalwart and powerful, broad in the beam like a seagoing tugboat. Its head is big even for such a massive body, its profile extending in a continuous sloping line to the end of the bill. The adult drake is spectacular in his harlequin plumage of sharply contrasting black and white, his body mainly black below and white above. Females and young males are golden brown covered with dark vermiculations.

Taking off is a laborious process for eiders. Once launched they fly low over the waves, not rising into the sky. Even on migration they fly in single file just above the water. They hunt their prey of molluscs and fish deep in the ocean, differing from other diving ducks in using their wings as well as their feet for propulsion. (When an eider plunges from the surface one sees its wings break open just as it disappears.)

On the Shetland moors, in some hollow of the ground without concealment, one would find a female on her eggs, her head resting on the grass to increase the inconspicuousness of her plumage against the background. Although one stood three feet away and returned the stare of her mild brown eye, she would not move or blink. In sheltered pools along the shores, and on some of the larger inland lochs, one found the females with up to five ducklings—often two females, with their respective broods, associated together. Like their mothers, the ducklings dove freely in search of food. Again, the proximity of human beings aroused nervousness but no alarm. (Here the enemy is not man but the Great Skua, which makes off with most of the ducklings that are hatched.) The incubation of eggs and the raising of young is all the work of the females, who have to stand such close guard against skuas and gulls that, before they have reached the stage of leading the ducklings to the water, they may have gone for days without eating at all.

Here and there along the shores, especially under the cliffs where the swells rose and broke down again, the drakes were gathered in rafts of thousands. Close in among the rocks that stood above the foaming surf— black rocks repeatedly scourged with lashings from which plumes of spray shot aloft—the drakes were swept violently back and forth with the wash of the water. They seemed always about to be flung up against the rocks and smashed.

Again, the scene was never of eiders alone; for there were all the gulls, Gannets, Shags, Fulmars, and alcids that filled the seascape in every direction. On the flatter

rocks the fat seals sprawled on their backs playing dead, flippers fallen apart. Sometimes the surface of the sea was broken by the triangular fins of Common Porpoises.

With the present explosive spread and development of man's dominion over the earth, other large species may survive, if at all, only in domestic or feral forms: either as the chattels of man, like farmyard geese, or as refugees from a defeated wilderness who, without becoming chattels, have still been able to find a place for themselves in his civilization—like the Brown Rat, the Gray Squirrel, the street pigeon, and the House Sparrow.

One species exists today in all three forms: wild, domestic, and feral. In its wild form it is the Rock Dove, which still nests here and there in caves or crevices of rock; in its domestic form it is the inmate of our dovecotes; in its feral form the pigeon of our city streets the world over.

Domestication of the wild Rock Dove is not of recent origin. In Norman times it was common practice in Britain "to erect platforms in the dove caves to facilitate the collection of squabs for immediate eating or for stocking the manorial dove-cotes."[1]

The street pigeon is a mongrel which has not yet found any final form of its own. Descended from domestic birds, some the weird products of the pigeon breeder's fancy, the tendency of these city birds to revert to the wild ancestral type—light gray, with two black wing-bars and a white rump—is blocked by two factors: (1) their genetic elements are constantly

[1] Murton and Clarke.

receiving new infusions of domestic stock, and (2) a dominant strain of melanism, eliminated by natural selection in the wild environment, persists in the urban environment, thereby producing a majority of dark birds.

The genetic transformation that responds to the new environment is not limited, however, to the replacement of light gray by sooty. Even those street pigeons that wear the colors of the wild Rock Dove do not compare with it in the trimness of its lines, in the sleekness of its plumage, in its alert bearing and the impression it gives of radiant vitality. They tend to be heavy and dowdy, and their flocks everywhere include those small, weak individuals, their feathers perpetually ruffled, that pigeon breeders call "runts."

The difference is of particular interest because it extends beyond this one species. It is the difference between what belongs to the wild and what belongs to our civilization; and so it applies as well to the House Sparrow, and to man himself. Inside the protecting walls of our civilization natural selection is not as stringent as outside; and it is natural selection, rejecting in each generation all except those who can meet the demands of an environment full of hazards, by contrast with the civilized environment, that has brought the wild Rock Dove to its perfection.

Where the wild Rock Dove still occurs, in sections of Europe and Asia, one cannot be sure, for the most part, that it has not acquired a significant amount of feral blood by miscegenation with feral pigeons, which are so widespread and abundant. There is a border zone in which feral and wild intergrade. The essential purity of the Shetland Rock Doves, however, is not in doubt. I daresay they quite outnumber the few feral pigeons to be found in Lerwick and some other settlements.

In the dark sea-caves where the Shags nest, where one sees them flying in and out, the Rock Doves also nest and are to be seen flying in and out. They are wild, wary, swift on the wing; and even at a distance, crossing the sky, one sometimes sees how the sunlight catches the irridescent stain on their necks. They represent the world as it may never be again. It is the street pigeons that, for better or worse, represent the successor world of man's dominion.

The Collared Dove, like the feral pigeon, has also adjusted to the great revolution in the history of our planet that is now reaching its culmination. It has abandoned the wild for the safety of human civilization and its amenities. Unlike the feral pigeon, however, it appears to have moved entirely on its own from the wilderness into the cities of men. Four centuries ago it had not yet spread from Asia Minor into Europe, except that it may already have become a city bird in the Istanbul of Suleiman the Magnificent. By the middle of the nineteenth century it had got no farther into Europe, as the town bird it now was, than Bulgaria.

Its real conquest of Europe, which is rapidly being completed today, did not get under way until our present century. In 1912 it first appeared in Belgrade; in 1930 it was spreading over southern Hungary; in 1943 it was at the gates of Vienna; on February 19, 1959 I got one of the first records of it for the Canton of Geneva, where it is now a common city bird; and when the *St. Clair* docked at Lerwick on July 1, 1968, it was perched on the roof of the dockside warehouse, as much at home as if it had not, in fact, just arrived from Asia Minor.

The feral pigeon and the Collared Dove—like the Mute Swan, the Gray Squirrel, the Brown Rat, and the House Mouse—belong to a new category of fauna, a category that after seven hundred million years of life on earth is now abruptly acquiring primary importance. They belong to the category of commensal creatures, creatures that have their place within human civilization and live in dependence on it.

The Starling, like the feral pigeon, is one of the most conspicuous of commensal birds. It belongs to the most evolved avian order, the *Passeriformes*, which is so far dominant that it contains over half the species of living birds (some 5,100 out of some 8,650) and, surely, the vast majority of individuals. Contrast this with the four species of relatively rare loons that constitute the whole of the primitive order *Gaviiformes*.

The starlings appear to have originated as a family of forest birds, but the common Starling came to find its principal source of food in the places where man had pastured cattle or planted grass; it came to find that man's buildings provided first-class nesting sites; and only lately it has discovered that the buildings along the busiest streets of his great metropolitan cities provide more attractive overnight roosts than what nature affords.

Men have deliberately introduced the Starling into North America, South Africa, Australia, and New Zealand, where it has spread and established itself at the expense of indigenous species. But even in its own native Europe, today, it is increasing and invading new regions, and apparently it is only in the present century that it has taken to roosting in its tens of thousands in the heart of London, where it seems to prefer the bright lights, the all-night traffic, and the incessant uproar of streets like the Haymarket. It reached Iceland in 1935 and appears to have got as far (at least provisionally) as Bear Island and Spitzbergen, high above the arctic circle, by the mid-1950s. In northern Scandinavia, to which it has recently spread, it appears to live in complete dependence on man.

This is not the case in Shetland, where one may still see the wild Starling of more primitive times living independent of human civilization, as one sees the ancestral form of our feral pigeon. In the dark sea-caves where the Shags and the Rock Doves are to be seen flying in and out, the Starlings are also to be seen flying in and out.

The Starling has been a native of Shetland so long that it has evolved a geographic variety confined to that archipelago and the Outer Hebrides, the sub-species *zetlandicus*. (The common European subspecies, *vulgaris*, inhabits Orkney, south of Shetland, and it would have been interesting to know to which of the two a lone Starling flying north over the sea halfway between Orkney and Shetland on the night of June 30/July 1, 1968 belonged.) It was recorded as abundant in Shetland in the 1790s; there is no reason to doubt that it was abundant in earlier centuries; and the Venables give it as their opinion that, of all the birds in Shetland today, it is the commonest. This special status that it has had so long here is the more interesting in that it did not colonize large parts of Scotland, to the south, until the middle of the last century. I speculate that the cliffs and caves of Shetland and the Outer Hebrides constituted a habitat to which it tended to be confined before the human habitat had reached a certain development.

Today the Starling is at home everywhere in Shetland, in every variety of habitat, with man and without man—no other bird so adaptable in its accommodation to different environments. A pair was nesting in the eaves of a cottage near the one we occupied, but we saw others flying in and out of caves and fissures of the sea-cliffs, where they were also nesting. They feed about the feet of the Shetland sheep and perch on their backs; but they may also associate themselves, in feeding, with Turnstones and Purple Sandpipers on the wild sea-beaches. The Starling, then, is both wild like the loon and commensal like the Collared Dove. And it is native to Shetland as the Collared Dove is not.

The most remarkable of all commensal birds is the House Sparrow. In the "Editor's Preface" to J. D. Summers-Smith's biography of the species it is referred to as probably the most abundant wild bird in the world today, with the possible exception of the Starling. Its abundance, however, is entirely due to its association with man. It has simply marched with him in the extension of his dominion. Its own consequent proliferation has matched his and, like his, continues today.

At the beginning of this commensal association the sparrow adapted itself to the habitat of agricultural man, living about his thatched huts or farm buildings, feeding with his pigs and poultry or in his grain fields. Mr. Summers-Smith reports, however, that "in many places the bird has emancipated itself from the agricultural background and is now largely associated with urbanized man." It has become a part of the urban community that includes man, the Brown Rat, and the feral pigeon—which, as we may well believe, will be the dominant community of the future on earth.

The parallel between the history of human civilization and the history of the sparrow is unique. Both began in the general area of the eastern Mediterranean. All the evidence indicates that the sparrow had its origin in ancestral weaver finches of tropical Africa, which spread down the Nile to the Mediterranean some ten to twenty million years ago (long before man had appeared on earth). Thence they began to spread along both shores of the Mediterranean. The last glaciation inhibited their continued spread, even imposed a retraction, and when it finally withdrew, some twenty-five thousand years ago, a portentous new ecological element appeared in the area between the Mediterranean and Caspian Seas, in the form of agricultural, grain-growing man, with whom the sparrows proceeded to associate themselves. They spread with man, then, across southern Asia and, beginning some five thousand years ago, northward into Europe. This northward spread in Europe, as well as the spread in Asia, is continuing apace today.

We know that the sparrow was a familiar bird in the north of England by the seventh century A.D. A thousand years later it had certainly reached Shetland, even though it was still only local in parts of Scotland and in the western half of the British Isles generally.

The explosive proliferation of its population, however, has taken place since the year 1800. It is still taking place, although it has already made the sparrow, according to Mr. Summers-Smith, "almost certainly the most widespread species of land bird in the world." For one thing, we men deliberately transported it across the oceans to North and South America, South Africa, Australia, and New Zealand. For another, of its own accord it followed the railway-line and the plow across Siberia to the Pacific. In the new continents the sparrows actually boarded railway-cars and traveled in them to regions where, like men, they proceeded to found new colonies. It is quite possible that, even if we men had not deliberately transported them across the oceans, they would have made it by themselves. Mr. Summers-Smith, reporting that a party of sparrows joined a ship at Bremerhaven, Germany, and disembarked from it at Melbourne, Australia, comments that "with this ability to traverse the oceans there must be few parts of the world denied to the bird."

The sparrows spread to the western isles of Scotland

in the late nineteenth century—although those of the islands that have since been abandoned by men have since been abandoned by them too. They reached Faroe, presumably by ship, in the mid-1930s. They crossed the arctic circle about the middle of the last century, and today they occur just south of the North Cape at 70° 40′ N. In these arctic regions, where they are thought to move from port to port in the ships in which they make themselves at home, they evidently depend almost entirely on food put out by man.

Meanwhile in Mexico they are spreading south, and in South America north, so that it appears but a matter of time before the two American populations meet and become one.

It is a fact, then, that the House Sparrows, having discovered the amenities of human civilization twenty-five thousand years ago, when that civilization was just beginning, have joined it and have established their place in it. They partake with man of his widening dominion. Not for them the fate of the Great Auk.

The subject of these chapters has been the birds of Shetland, which include the Storm Petrel and the Starling, the Red-throated Loon and the House Sparrow. Their theme, however, has been the catastrophically changing relationship, in our present, between man and the primitive world of nature to which the birds have hitherto belonged.

In that world, and under the discipline of natural selection, for something like a hundred and sixty million years the class *Aves* has developed the wide variety of forms we know today, and has been perfecting those forms. The beauty of the Fulmar, of the Red-necked Phalarope, of the Arctic Skua, of the Black Guillemot, of the Gannet, and of the Rock Dove is a consequence of their having been engaged for a hundred and sixty thousand millennia in a process of self-realization. Each has been realizing the quintessential self that was potential in its beginnings. Each has been evolving toward the perfection of what it is.

Man has been on earth only a million years, and his own self-realization is less advanced. This gives point to D. H. Lawrence's statement that, if a man were as much of a man as a lizard is a lizard, he would be more worth looking at.

The self-realization of species in their own perfection has hitherto depended on the natural environment that has imposed its own harsh discipline of natural selection. Now, however, man in the course of his own self-realization is replacing this environment with an artificial environment in which natural selection is less rigorous. For a century past, ever since we discovered the principle of natural selection, we men have speculated that the exemption from its former rigors provided by our developing civilization might result in a degeneration, at least in some respects, of our kind. The survival and proliferation of individuals who could not survive in a state of nature is bound to have its consequences, although we are more ignorant of what they may be than we readily admit.

This is not, however, a problem for man alone. The street pigeon, protected from predators and the elements as its wild forebears were not, has visibly changed in that it is not as strong, swift, and alert as the Rock Dove that represents the original stock. By criteria that have a philosophical rather than a scientific basis (discussed in the Epilogue), it has fallen away from the perfection to which the Rock Dove still holds.

In our cities the House Sparrow, too, is protected from predators and, living as it does at man's table, has to spend remarkably little time in foraging for food, even during the cold northern winters. In consequence, it has gained an extraordinary amount of the leisure that is a prime benefit of civilization for man as well. Its unique success among all birds up to now, like the unique success of man among the beasts, testifies to the advantages of the civilization that man and sparrow share. There has, however, been loss too. The sparrow shows some of the same elements of degeneration as the street pigeon. Of all the Shetland birds that take one's breath away by the perfection of their beauty, whether of form or movement, the sparrows of the Lerwick streets are by common consent the least beautiful.

Finally, the problem of our own future in an artificial environment exempt from the more stringent requirements of the natural environment is the same for all those species that, if they are to survive at all in a world remodeled by man, will be able to do so only as his wards, cared for by him like the remnant herds of degenerate bison in national parks of the United States and Canada.

In the last few centuries our spreading human population has taken over virtually the entire earth. At the same time, however, it has been concentrating its numbers in the great new urban complexes that it has been creating. The result in many areas, exemplified by Shetland, has been a depopulation of the countryside that, continuing, could at last be virtually total.

We cannot foresee the future but we can recognize our responsibilities. In consequence of the establishment of our dominion, the wildlife of the earth today faces a crisis unmatched in the thousands of millions of years of its evolution. Its various species must either find places for themselves in the new world of human making or perish. Our responsibility is, by deliberate forethought, to help them find such places. In some instances we will be able to take them indoors: our civilization will be able to accommodate them, as it accommodates the House Sparrow, without making any special provision. In others, some such provision will have to be made as is now made in Europe for the Mute Swan. If, however, our entire human population ends by moving, at last, into the urban conglomerations so rapidly forming today, then the consequent depopulation of the countryside, as in Shetland, offers the hope that many wild species may be enabled to survive in their integrity. In that case, the disappearance or degeneration of the wild world, still so radiantly represented in Shetland, need not be absolute. And in that case the observations which I here conclude need not be valedictory.

To know that what is impenetrable to us really exists, manifesting itself as the highest wisdom and the most radiant beauty, which our dull faculties can comprehend only in their most primitive forms—this knowledge, this feeling, is at the center of true religiousness. In this sense, and in this sense only, I belong to the ranks of devoutly religious men.

IX. EPILOGUE

WHEN the first chapter of *Genesis* was written about the ninth century B.C., the men who set it down thought the universe hardly more extensive than the world they perceived directly with their senses. There was heaven above and earth below. Heaven contained the sun, the moon, and the stars, all of which had been created for no other purpose than to light the earth. Upon the earth there had been created categories and sub-categories of life: vegetable life, the herb yielding seed and the fruit tree yielding fruit after their kind; animal life, first that of the sea, the great whales and every living creature that moved in the sea after its kind, then that of the air, every winged fowl after its kind, then that of the land, cattle after their kind and every thing that crept upon the earth after its kind. Finally, to crown all, the Creator had created man in his own image to have dominion over the fish of the sea, the fowl of the air, and every living thing that moved upon the earth.

Since then we have learned that the earth is only one satellite circling the sun, which is merely as one of some fifty thousand million specks of dust in a galaxy a hundred thousand light-years across (so that light traveling at 186,000 miles-per-second takes that many years to cross it), which in turn is merely one of millions of galaxies that extend across thousands of millions of light-years to realms of space beyond our knowing. In terms of this physical universe it is less sure that man is, as we once thought, the appointed lord of creation.

We have also learned since *Genesis* that life is not divided into separate, unrelated categories and sub-categories: a vegetable kingdom and an animal kingdom, each with its several species, and as sovereign over both kingdoms, in a class by himself, man. If viruses are living organisms, as most biologists regard them, then they cannot be classified as belonging to either of the two kingdoms into which we had supposed all non-human life to be divided; and we must in any case suppose that the division we make between vegetable and animal did not arise until after the first stages of the evolution of life on earth.

More than that, because there is some doubt that viruses are living beings at all, they might represent an intermediate link between non-living and living matter. We cannot know that, tracing life back from the more developed to the increasingly primitive, there is any line at which it ceases to be, even though it becomes so tenuous at last that we can no longer detect its presence—which is to say that the element of life may exist even in atoms and their constituent particles.

At the other end of the scale of evolution, we can no longer regard any species, man included, as a separate creation. Man's ancestry goes back without a break through earlier anthropoids, through more primitive mammals, through the reptiles from which

the mammals developed—back to some speck of organic matter that may itself have arisen out of atoms
joined in combinations that we would not recognize
as representing living matter at all. And the line of
the Rock Dove's ancestry, traced back, would join with
the line of man's ancestry at some point in evolution
beyond which, going backwards in time, man and
dove have a common ancestry.

We can trace the evolution of life back over some
three and a half thousand million years to the oldest
organic fossils now known, some minute alga-like
spheroids—but who knows how much further back it
may go, or even whether, latent in all matter, it does
not go back to times before the birth of our solar
system? Tracing this evolutionary history back in
time, our categories disappear as such. There is no
line to be drawn between man and an earlier hominid
—that is, no hominid female of another species giving
birth to the first man, *Homo sapiens*, a new species.
There is no line to be drawn between prehominid
anthropoids and hominids—no non-hominid couple
that were parents of the first hominid. Similarly, there
is no line to be drawn between mammals and reptiles,
between animal and vegetable, perhaps between ani-
mate and inanimate. If one's vision could encompass
all time, then all life from the beginning, and perhaps
all being, would be seen as a continuum on which we
mark artificial gradations as we mark degrees centi-
grade on a thermometer to measure changes of temperature that do not, however, proceed by the categorical jumps our marks represent.

Considering this, there is a paradox in the fact that
the predominant ontological thought since Hegel has
given man the same importance in the universe as he
had in the first chapter of *Genesis*. I explain this by the
fact that the post-Hegelian philosophers have lived
their lives in a closed environment, in the great urban
conglomerations which were beginning to develop for

the first time in Karl Marx's day. Marx moved from one city to another, unobservant of what lay between them. He was blind to the aboriginal world of nature, to the multitude of species other than man which represented that world. He was unconcerned with the thousands of millions of years of life on earth that had preceded the five thousand years of man's recorded history. He was unconcerned with the outer space in which our planet appears so small. All of significant reality to him was Cologne or Brussels, Paris or London—examples of a narrow and isolating environment, like that of the beehive for the bee, within which man appears as the sole creator. The same could be said for such a typical philosopher of our own day as Mr. Jean-Paul Sartre, to whom all reality, one sometimes suspects, is a café in Paris. In this environment a tree exists only in consequence of a decision by the municipal authorities.

The general acceptance by the intellectual world of the limited vision represented by Marx and Sartre is explicable in the same terms. The dominant intellectual communities of our time inhabit the same closed environment, not taking seriously the fact of a world beyond it.

In one way this man-centered point of view, which has its ironical resemblance to that of *Genesis*, has a justification in actuality, the justification that the wild Honey Bee would have in regarding this as a world made by bees and for bees if their beehives should at last spread to cover the earth. It is true that today man has gained dominion over the little planet on which we live, which he is rapidly making over into a world for man. A world for man, then, presents itself to the inhabitants of the closed environment as the only justifiable purpose of being, of creation itself. They do not want to look beyond it. To them I have nothing I can say, as I know only too well. The rest of this epilogue is addressed, therefore, to those who feel the narrowness and oppression of confinement, in mind and imagination, to the urban equivalent of the bee-hives within which the majority of our kind are enclosing themselves.

Considering the size of the universe and the small-ness of our kind in it, I cannot suppose that all its meaning (and there is no rational way of doubting that it does have meaning) is summed up in us and our destiny. We are only one among countless passing manifestations of life on this one planet, not to speak of the life we may suppose to exist elsewhere; and life itself is only one aspect of a nature that extends so far beyond our knowledge.

In the midst of this vastness I am like the blind mole feeling his way through the underground darkness of the sphere to which he is limited. Even within this sphere, however, I am aware of a dynamic tension between opposites that I must suppose to be universal. It is the tension between disorder and order, between imperfection and perfection, between the ugly and the beautiful.

What I now say I shall confine to life as we know it on our planet, although I find no difficulty in sup-posing it to be applicable to the great cosmos itself. The tension to which I have referred is dynamic be-cause all life, in its evolution, is driven by an im-pulsion to bring order out of disorder, to overcome its own imperfections, to realize itself in its own per-fection. Thus life, of which man is one expression, has drive and direction.

I apply this to the evolution of species, including our own. The mechanics of that evolution, in so far as they are known to us, are those of natural selection for fitness to whatever the environment may be in which it operates at a particular place and time. In all species, genetic mutations occur at random. Those that increase fitness are perpetuated, thereby cumulatively increasing the total fitness of the species. If the environment of a species never changed, it would, by this process, ultimately achieve the nearest possible approach to total fitness in terms of that environment. As environments change, however, so do the criteria of fitness and the consequent direction of evolution for those species that survive the change.

All of us pedagogues, spending our lives in communication with the young who have come to us for the knowledge they lack, are unconsciously impelled to impress them with the supposed authority, completeness, and finality of the knowledge for which we are the professional spokesmen. We therefore tend to avoid drawing attention to what is unknown or uncertain, and to dismiss without really answering any questions that tend to uncover our real ignorance. Each generation of students is brought up, as I was, on the distinction between "what people used to believe" and "what we now know." What passes in each generation, however, for "what we now know" is what will be taught to future generations as "what people used to believe." So it is that, in the orthodoxy represented by textbooks, the theory of natural selection based on random or accidental mutations is still given, today, as the whole explanation of the evolution of species. Biologists ever since Darwin himself, however, have in fact been uncertain of the basis on which selection occurs.

The rediscovery after Darwin's day of Mendelian theory led to the theory of random mutations in the genes as the basis. That such mutations occur is not in question. That they constitute one important basis for natural selection is not in question. What is in question is that the theory is by itself adequate to explain the whole evolution of life, from the most primitive original speck to the most elaborately organized organisms and associations of organisms known in our own times.

In fact, there are organisms and relationships that cannot be convincingly explained by it. Besides the reluctance of all of us to acknowledge ignorance, there is another reason, related to it, why this is not mentioned in the textbooks or bruited by the majority of ordinary biologists. We are all powerfully impelled to adhere to an old theory, however demonstrable its inadequacies, until a new theory has become available for its replacement. This represents our human horror of the unknown recognized as such, the horror of living with phenomena for which no explanation, not even a specious one, is available. Thus physicists adhered to Newtonian theory, in spite of a growing body of phenomena that could not be explained in terms of it, until Einstein had provided an alternative theory to which they could adhere. (This alternative theory also has its inadequacies today, but is fiercely defended in the absence, as yet, of still another alternative.) Sir Peter Medawar, himself a distinguished scientist, has written: "Scientists tend not to ask themselves questions until they can see the rudiments of an answer in their minds. Embarrassing questions tend to remain unasked or, if asked, to be answered rudely."[1]

I cannot here argue extensively the case for doubt, but I shall give one example of the kind of circumstances, not uncommon, on which it is in part based. There are many species of the plant genus *Yucca*, each of which depends entirely for its reproduction on a species of moth, the Yucca Moth, which in turn depends for its own reproduction and survival entirely on the yucca with which it is thus associated. The moth has a special organ between its jaws, which other moths lack, for collecting the yucca's pollen. The yucca produces flowers that are open at most for one night per year, and not always every year. The female

[1] London, 1960, p. 62. (Quoted by Hardy.)

of the moth can do her part only when she is ready to lay eggs, which must be at the time when the yucca flowers are open. She then uses her special organ to collect a ball of pollen from one yucca flower, which she carries in flight to another yucca flower. At the second flower, using another specialized organ, she cuts a hole in the bottom of the pistil, inside which she then lays one or several eggs. That done, she climbs up the pistil and places the pollen ball on the stigma, thereby fertilizing the flower. The seeds that, in consequence of this fertilization, are produced at the bottom of the pistil, where the eggs were layed as if by foresight, are the only food on which the larvae hatched from the eggs can live, but a sufficient number are formed to reproduce the plant as well as feed the larvae.

There are years when no yuccas bloom at all over as wide an area as the moths can travel, but the moths escape consequent extirpation because, when that happens, their larvae continue for another year in the chrysalis, changing into moths only when the yuccas again bloom.

The thesis that this symbiotic relationship came about entirely by random mutations in the genes of the yucca's and the moth's respective ancestors, and the selection of their respective mutations by the criterion of relative fitness, strains credulity. Was a random mutation the cause by which the first moth was impelled to enter into the relationship by doing anything as seemingly senseless as deliberately to collect pollen from one yucca flower and transport it to another? Was it the same mutation or another that caused it, at the same time, to lay its eggs at a point on the yucca where the larvae that hatched could profit from the seeds consequently produced? And did these mutations then manifest themselves in more and more moths, causing them deliberately to commit this seemingly senseless combination of acts because of the advantage they thereby conferred in terms of fitness? And did the yucca's ancestor, at the same time, produce mutations at random that complimented the mutations in the moth? Did the two species evolve in close coordination with each other to such a far-reaching extent entirely on the basis of complimentary mutations that occurred at random in each separately? Was the whole process carried forward by a natural selection that responded blindly to haphazard factors in the environment? There are reputable biologists who cannot bring themselves to answer these questions affirmatively.

This is not the place to multiply such examples. The reader can find others in books by quite a few dissenting authorities of good reputation, e.g., in Chapter VIII of Sir Alister Hardy's Gifford Lectures, published in 1965.

My own scepticism of what I may call textbook theory did not originate with my reading of the dissident literature to which I have just referred. It troubled me when, many years ago, I first read Darwin's *The Various Contrivances by which Orchids are Fertilized by Insects*. Here he describes, for species after species, the excessively specialized and elaborate devices on which orchids, the most highly evolved of monocotyledonous plants, have come to depend for their reproduction. What struck me was that these devices are so complex and delicate, depending on such a sequence of contingencies in each case, that for the most part they do not work. In most cases the process from pollenization to the production of a new generation is simply not accomplished. There are too many points at which it can fail because some peculiar circumstance on which it depends is lacking. More primitive plants with much cruder, less evolved devices for reproduction, like the *Ranunculaceae* (to which our buttercups belong), are far more successful than the orchids. Surely this at least raises a question, which needs to be answered, about fitness as the sole criterion of selection. Is there some other good that, in these cases, overrides fitness?

The same question is raised by countless examples in nature of specialized forms, produced by the process of evolution, that would appear to be actually disadvantageous to survival in any environment. Think of the birds that make themselves conspicuous, and therefore vulnerable to predators, by acquiring brightly colored plumage in the breeding season—our Scarlet Tanager for example. It is not enough to say that this makes them more intimidating to rivals of their own species or more attractive to their mates, for these psychological factors are, themselves, the supposed products of selection based on fitness for survival. In some cases one is tempted to speculate that evolutionary processes may somehow acquire a momentum of their own that carries them beyond the optimum in terms of such fitness.

My point in making these observations is simple. We have a theory of evolution that is good as far as it goes, but that is doubtful as the sole and complete explanation of the course evolution has taken and the results it has produced. We continue to accept it and teach it as the sole and complete explanation, telling the young that it is quite satisfactory, because we have as yet no confirmed new theory with which to supplement if not replace it. In such circumstances I claim only the right to speculate beyond the bounds of orthodoxy, as well as the possible utility of doing so.[2]

I return, then, to a teleological vein of speculation. There is an impulsion in all life, and perhaps in all being, toward self-perfection in terms of criteria im-

---

[2] I. M. Lerner (1958) writes: "At this stage of our knowledge it may be pardonable to be vague about the details of the means by which macro-evolutionary changes may be expected to be brought about. It is clear that unorthodox approaches are needed." (Quoted by T. A. Goudge, p. 131.)

plicit in the constitution of the universe, in creation itself.[3] This is the basis of aesthetic perception. It is the basis of what Einstein called "the highest wisdom and the most radiant beauty," which he also referred to as "this knowledge, this feeling, [which] is at the center of true religiousness." It is the significance of what presents itself to us as "order" and as "logic." It is what Socrates was expressing in his theory of "forms" or "ideas." It is what Chinese philosophers meant by the *tao*. It is what the author of the Gospel according to John meant by the *logos*. It is what St. Paul preached. It is what Kant meant by the noumenal. It is what Hegel saw as the goal of the evolution of all being. Since Hegel's day, and the rise to dominance of positivistic thinking, it has gone out of fashion. But fashions in thought are evanescent. They have never had any serious relevance to truth, the search for which is always subversive in terms of orthodoxy and fashion alike.

The difficulty is in seeing how, in operative terms, a tendency toward self-perfection would produce changes in the genes. One answer has been suggested by molecular biologists who have argued that, quite apart from selection by the environment, there is what they call internal selection. The case for this is argued by Lancelot Law Whyte. Every organism has an internal order (involving its atoms, ions, molecules,

---

[3] I have argued the case for this at book-length in my *Men and Nations*. The assumption that the universe, in its evolution, is realizing a pre-existing purpose, which is what teleological thinking generally implies, is so unfashionable today that thinkers are driven to deny that they have any such thoughts even as their predecessors in the Middle Ages were driven to deny any association with heresy. But evolution could be regarded as moving in the direction of ever higher values, by the criterion of a philosophy that attaches value to some kind of logical order, without that direction representing a pre-established end or purpose. See Blum, pp. 195-7, where he distinguishes between direction and purpose.

organelles, etc.) to which any genetic mutation must conform if it is to survive and find expression in the phenotype that is then exposed to environmental (i.e. external) selection. Some mutations are thus rejected because they do not fit into the structural order—which is another way of saying that some are selected for their conformity to the structural order—before Darwinian selection can operate upon them. Under some circumstances, in which there has been no excess of population over what the environment can accommodate, environmental selection has been largely inoperative, so that evolution has then been directed largely by internal selection, which is always operative.

The concept of internal selection provides no answer to the problem posed by such symbiotic relationships as that between the yuccas and the Yucca Moth. Whyte, moreover, does not regard internal selection as orthogenic, since it may follow many avenues of potential evolution. I myself, however, wonder whether one could not conceive the possibility that these factors, responding to a basic order, so narrowed down the choice of direction that the evolution of any particular form could take as to approach a situation of orthogenesis. Whyte predicts that the process of evolution will be found to show "an inherent tendency towards order."[4]

Following my vein of teleological speculation, then, I am impressed by the aesthetic element in the evolution of nature. (Here I am associating aesthetic appreciation in man with the basic order I have postulated.) The orchids may not represent a greater fitness in terms of survival, but they are more beautiful than more primitive plants. They impress us as being more complete in terms of an ideal perfection. Again, we know that birds sing to inform other individuals belonging to their species that they are on their own

[4] Page 73.

territory, which they will defend against trespass. But this is as readily achieved by those species that simply croak as by the Nightingale, which is moved to engage in a performance at once elaborate, inventive, and as beautiful in its way as a sonata by Mozart. If year after year, as I do, one hears the Nightingales in their neighboring territories obviously competing in song, each driven to improvise creatively on the basis of aesthetic standards that we can recognize—with diminuendos, crescendos, accelerandos, ritardandos—the existence of a drive in all life toward the progressive realization of an idea of perfection becomes, at least, plausible. The territorial theory, which I do not question, tells me why the Nightingale sings at all. It does not tell me why it sings beautifully.

Like the blind mole I speculate on what is beyond my knowledge, what is as yet beyond the knowledge of us all. I feel in myself, and I see in the history of humanity and in the evolution of all life, an impulse to overcome chaos, to realize an order implicit in being. This is what we call the creative impulse in our poets, our artists, our musicians. But it is not confined to them, for they have audiences who also respond to it, and it does not separate our species from the great stream of all life, from nature itself, in which the creative impulse may be seen as the spring of being. To recognize it is, it seems to me, constructive, while to deny it is the basis of the nihilism that, in the periods of our decadence, moves us toward cultural self-destruction. The polarity I originally referred to is everywhere, so that inside each of us chaos, destruction, and death confront the demands of creativity. Their appeal represents a natural reaction against the burden of such demands, a reaction that in particular societies at particular times becomes dominant.

Every individual has the impulse to realize his own self-perfection. Every species is under the drive to realize the self-perfection of its kind. Life itself, and perhaps all being, is driven to realize the perfection of an order that we experience only in imperfection. I suppose that something like this, embracing life as a whole, represents the purpose or meaning of the universe—something like this, rather than a world of material well-being for men of dulled senses confined to prisons of their own construction, the rest of nature shut out as the non-apian world is excluded from the beehive.

These thoughts are relevant to the responsibility that has become ours with the achievement, in our time, of the dominion over nature, within the confines of our planet, that was promised in *Genesis*. A petty humanitarianism seems to me not enough. We need a reverence for life in all its forms, for nature, for the beauty that has been achieved so painfully over thousands of millions of years in the small sphere that is our native earth. The vision of the urban philosopher, which excludes the Storm Petrel, is too narrow for the responsibilities that have become ours.

Evolution or history has at last given us dominion over the earth: over the herb yielding seed and the fruit tree yielding fruit after its kind; over the fowl that fly above the earth in the open firmament of heaven; over the great whales and every living creature that moveth, which the waters brought forth abundantly after their kind; over every thing that creepeth upon the earth after its kind. It is a remarkable fact that, so long after *Genesis* was written, and in circumstances so different and yet so similar to those of the Garden of Eden, man should at last have achieved this dominion. Surely this implies a responsibility that must be based on love, and on a consequent respect for the whole of life in terms of its self-perfecting dynamism.

PART TWO

OF BIRDS
AND BOUNDARIES

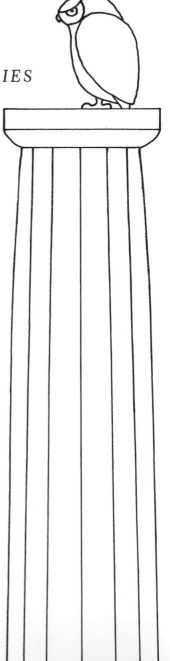

THE WATER RAIL

In 1956, as I was about to move across the Atlantic, an American publisher suggested that I write a book of observations on man and nature in Europe, similar to one I had written on man and nature in America called Spring in Washington. *I had no mind simply to attempt a repetition in a new setting of what I had done in the old. Instead, as I looked about here and there in Europe, I set down such odd thoughts and casual observations of birds and men as came into my head. After a year or two, when I had accumulated enough pages for a sample, I sent them to the publisher. His response brought me to earth with a bump. He pointed out that what I was writing did not belong to any of the categories for which there was a market in the American book-trade. So I brought the whole enterprise to an abrupt halt—right in the middle of a paragraph that will remain forever unfinished.*

WE HAVE a Water Rail in our front yard.

It comes out of the reeds after it has assured itself that no one is looking. Delicately. One foot forward and down. Then the other. Picks lightly at the mud, first here, then there, leaning forward. Twitches up its hind end repeatedly, a nervous habit, showing white beneath the tail in flashes. From a distance what appears is only an obscure body with flashes off and on— at what looks like the head end. (Tail is up, generally, real head down.) Perhaps it fools enemies that way. Jump at it, if you are lustful, and it takes off backward! The hawk or the cat sits foolish, not knowing what has happened.

We have a mud-bank only in spring. Like a Water Rail disappearing into the reeds the Lake of Geneva recedes gradually. The flat wet mud, ready for toe-prints, separates the low embankment wall at the edge of our lawn from the restless edge of the lake, which runs up in ripples repeating, repeating, trying again and again. (You never see them withdraw. So much in this world is hidden and deceptive!)

The situation in France is clouded and variable. I don't suppose the Water Rail ever looks that far from its home-ground between lake and lawn. The Jura Mountains are beyond picking distance of its bill. Anyway, it wouldn't understand. But I, with my superb brain, my global vision, cast my gaze across the lake and above the opposite shore to where the clouded and variable situation of France presents itself. The Water Rail just picks the mud.

The Moorhens must be the superiors of the Water Rail. At least they are bigger, darker, and bolder (though timid). There are two. In addition to picking at the mud and making the same white flashes with their tails they swim. The Water Rail joins them but runs away again if they look at it. All three are forever ready to slip into the reeds, becoming nothing. (Maybe it is just an illusion that, out of the reeds, they are something.)

I can count on the Coot, which are countless. Bigger, blacker, with white Roman noses instead of tails, innumerable, confident in the open lake swimming and diving, or flying with legs dangling. Jump at them and—pop, they are underwater. Wait and—pop, they are up again. Water Rails and Moorhens never pop at all, one way or the other. They fade like the Cheshire cat, leaving behind them a suspicion that they never were there at all.

The Coot yap like toy dogs. The rail, I am told, emits those quick successive squeels and cries of pain that sometimes come from the reeds at dusk. It must be up to something it shouldn't be doing. But I never saw what.

Still the situation in France remains clouded.

✧

Five Velvet Scoters bob close together in the bay of Hermance, the border village. Atlantic sea ducks, these, who must be in the heart of Europe by mistake. They haven't read the books that tell where they should go for each season. They go where they please, undisciplined.

We are in Switzerland, they in France. We must obtain the agreement of two countries (two nation-states of the twentieth century) if we are to see them closer. The gray border-guard nods his head, for his country, and we stalk past him after scoters. (Switzerland agrees.) The guard in blue sits by the fat iron stove in his hut. He belongs to an old civilization. He will not come out in cold weather—not for scoters, not for scoterists. France agrees by default—unless there was an affirmative movement of the eyelids. (So much in this world is hidden and deceptive!) We make a little voyage around France now, a country where Velvet Scoters find themselves. But the scoters take off, objecting to sharing the same country with us, and enter Switzerland without permission.

Monsieur P., who inhabits Hermance, tells the gray guard that he is often to be seen proceeding up that wagon-track (over there) into France. He wishes to explain that it is not to smuggle cigarettes but for birds. If, for example, he is seen this same night on the brow of that hill, entering or leaving France, his silhouette against the sky, it is for the *bécasse*. (The *bécasse* is the Woodcock, which has come early this year and settled in a valley of the Haute-Savoie several hundred meters away.)

"*Service,*" says the guard, saluting.

✧

The political situation sometimes gives the bird an advantage. Later in the season I find myself in the Bois de Jussy following the song of a Song Thrush across a vegetable garden. (But where is the singer?) The Canton and Republic of Geneva, which is rich in many things, is not rich in Song Thrushes. You have to go to the Bois de Jussy, at its edge, to hear them.

Now if this one would retreat up the little road into France all would be well. I don't mind following him past the two guards, one always on each side of the frontier. Each would be glad to see me in this lonely place, and the only thing might be that they would want to converse, where here was I on the trail of a thrush who would not wait. Still, that would be one thing. But to leave the little road in the dusk and, crouching, cross the border through someone's vegetable garden. . . . This is suspicious behavior.

An honest man should never feel guilty. But what would you? (French shrug of the shoulders here: *Que voulez-vous?*) We are none of us born honest. So we must keep up appearances against Original Sin. No one must know.

If this were a Blue Rock-thrush, that would be one thing. No. I have decided. I shall not follow the musician (*la musicienne*) out of this country. Here I am safe. Here I am happy. Here I have my *permis d'établissement.*

✧

At Chancy, the frontier-post down the Rhône, the Swiss guard makes us pass an examination. But he has only one question.

"Did you know that those two birds you were looking at were *goélands* [gulls]?"

"*Oui, Monsieur, goélands argentés* [Herring Gulls].

"*Passez, Messieurs!*"

✧

Sometimes a border-guard will ask: "Do you have

anything to declare?" He is speaking for France, or for Switzerland. What an opportunity!

Do I have anything to declare? *Do* I have anything to declare? I should say I do! Listen, France! Listen, Switzerland! . . .

But my throat and chest are suddenly jammed up with all I have to declare. For the moment nothing comes out. The guard mistakes my silence for a negative and waves us on.

✧

My subject is the Water Rail, but speaking about borders . . .

Johnny and I have a scooter and are scooterists. Being nine years old Johnny rides pillion, but counts the days till he is twice as old and may lawfully seize control for himself. It is an Italian motor-scooter, a Lambretta. On it he and I have crossed the high Jura in snow and ice (once, at high speed, spilling and sprawling on a lovely curve). (You travel on an icy pavement by sliding both feet along the ground, even at fifty-kilometers-an-hour, keeping the machine up that way.) On it we have dashed to distant places, for a look at birds, and back again in time for lunch. It is our true love.

On the scooter, one day, we visited the last city-state. The fall of Rome was accompanied by the rise of San Marino, as by the rise of Venice. The Venetians took refuge on the lagoons of the Adriatic from the triumphant barbarians. The Sanmarinese took refuge on a rock. It rises sheer, like a dream, from the plains behind Rimini. But Venice was importantly involved in the world, and when the Atlantic became navigable she declined. Today she is a city in Italy. San Marino is still an independent city-state, as important as it has ever been.

I lecture Johnny (being bigger than he is). There is the city—towers, turrets, and battlements—trimming the top of the rock that stands above green fields. The green fields are the surrounding and supporting land in which the food is grown. When invaders attack, the fields may be burned, but the population has found refuge within the city walls. Just like Athens and Corinth, like Pylos and Sparta, like Siena, Pisa, and Florence. Just like the original Rome on its seven hills. *Nota bene!* End of lecture. (Johnny continues to think of lizards.)

We see no Italian guards at the frontier. But across it are two grandly dressed Sanmarinese (looking like Mandarin Ducks, *Aix galericulata*). We slow up for a stop. They regard us bewildered, wondering whether we are stopping to question them. Having no questions (unless to ask whether they want to question us), we speed up again, plunging headlong into the Republic of San Marino, toward the citadel, toward the steep road zigzagging up to it. Since we always climb every tower we are allowed to, Johnny and I shall be occupied in San Marino this afternoon.

Coming back in the evening there are no guards on either side of the border. San Marino sleeps. Italy sleeps. Mars sleeps.

✧

Not far from the last city-state is another frontier, the crossing of which changed the history of the world. Scooting down the Via Aemilia from Forli to Rimini we come to a little bridge with a little sign: *Fiume Rubicone*. A terrible decision must be made. We stop the scooter and pull it off the road near a gas-station, getting it out of danger from the heedless trucks. The Rubicon flows along the bottom of a declivity. With only one steppingstone we could cross it dryshod and have no need of a bridge.

While history remains in suspense, while the Fates themselves hold their breath, Johnny clambers down the side of the declivity to hunt for lizards. The responsibility is on me, and I remain pondering. . . .

At last Johnny returns. We say nothing, but the decision has been taken. Grimly we board the scooter. I no longer hesitate. The time is 2:07 p.m. on April 15, 1957. At full throttle we cross the Rubicon. Turning to John I cry: "The die is cast!" (which means: *Alea jacta est!*).

A few minutes later we carry the eagles into Rimini.

✧

I cannot understand John's absorption in lizards. The mystery first impressed itself on me one afternoon when we stood amid the ruins of Ostia, the seaport and beach of ancient Rome. All about us are the remains of villas, baths, academies, theaters, temples; marble columns broken and unbroken; vaulted roofing here and there; often second or third stories to which one can climb; the whole in rolling pasture where shepherds with staffs (but no pipes) tend sheep and the flat-topped pines give blots of shade. (In classical lands these trees are flat-topped; they are spires in gothic lands.) What great thoughts are called for here, here where the Roman patricians once resorted to escape vulgar Rome, to enjoy high society by the sea! . . .

But John is absorbed in trying to catch a lizard that has escaped him among the loose bricks of a staircase. No use saying anything to him. He would not hear, or would pretend not to hear. It comes as a great thought that this is the world of one's own loneliness. . . .

Across the open atrium a flash and suddenly a little bird on a brick-pile—on its toes, alert, bobbing repeatedly. I lift my binoculars to my eyes and call out: "John! Quickly! A Wheatear!" (He does not hear, so intense is his lizarding.) Now another bird flying low, undulating, in and out among the ruins, hidden, again seen. Lands on a low pedestal and freezes. Sunlight perfect on it, from behind me. "John! Quick! A Rock Thrush!"

By this time I have crossed the atrium and a court-yard beyond. I have come to the low wire-fence at the edge of the ruins. In the sheep pasture beyond are other birds, a pair of warblers that are either White-throats or Lesser Whitethroats. I cross the fence. (Johnny forgotten now.) Farther along, a small bird lands upright against a fencepost and twists its head outlandishly, wryly, to look at me. My first Wryneck! . . .

Half an hour later, when I had made my way back to the staircase, I found John as absorbed as ever in his effort to catch the lizard. Here were all the ruins of Ostia about him, here lay the greatest civilization that ever fell, and all he could think about was lizards!

❖

Going to Ostia we had to inquire our way. But, re-turning, we did not ask which road led to Rome.

❖

A scooter is the only means of getting about Rome. The big automobiles and the little pedestrians alike hardly have a chance.

On the Via Venezia the traffic policeman throws up his hand to stop the traffic. It keeps on going. He makes a quarter turn and beckons the cross traffic to come on. It comes on. He sees a clash imminent and throws up his hand for the cross traffic not to come on after all. Still it comes on. The next moment every-thing meets in the middle and everything has to stop. The two streams of traffic are locked into each other and, since nothing can be done, the policeman shrugs his shoulders and laughs. (In Italy they know how to relax.)

This is your scooter's moment. You half walk it, half ride it, between the imprisoned cars, meandering, cross the intersection through the thick of the jam and keep on going. Nothing imprisons a scooter.

'Vantage Number One! You couldn't do that in a Cadillac.

✦

At every grade-crossing the barricades go down ten minutes, perhaps fifteen minutes before train-time. The line of stopped cars lengthens on either side. Drivers get out to stretch and smoke. Along we come, past the one line of cars; get off and, crouching to pass under the bars, walk the scooter across the tracks; board again and roar on, past the other line of cars. (The drivers cast longing and envious looks.)

'Vantage Number Two! You couldn't do that in a Cadillac.

✦

I, the neighbor of a Water Rail, have been a pedestrian in mediaeval Florence. The mob is compressed in the narrow streets, but through the mash automobiles and scooters force their way. Here even scooters must go so slowly that, when one hooks a button on your sleeve, you may have time to unhook it before it is taken off.

In the middle of the Ponte Vecchio Johnny and I are carried forward and back by the mob, from side to side. I keep hold of his hand as one does with a child in the surf. This is the old Ponte Vecchio, I tell myself, of which I have seen so many pictures, of which I must again look at a picture.

Still holding Johnny's hand, I am thrown up against a lady I had known elsewhere. She shouts at me something that sounds like "Isn't it charming?"

"What?" I shout back, cupping my ear.

"Isn't it charming? . . . "Is-n't it char-ming?"

"Yes" is all I have a chance to shout. (Just as well.) I have to attend to John, down below. He wants to know when we get to the Ponte Vecchio.

✦

But even Florence is not too bad if you are properly mounted. On a scooter you can cut through the crowd like a dull knife through heavy cheese.

✧

We have gone to the Museum of St. Mark especially to look at Fra Angelico's "Last Judgment." I want to show John the detail, in one corner, of the blessed dancing in a ring (though I know he is more interested in the damned). But other visitors are ahead of us, standing in a broken shifting mass before the painting. Occasionally there are openings—but they close up again too quickly. Later, in a shop window, I find a reproduction and am able to show John the dancers.

✧

We stand on the Leaning Tower of Pisa and watch two silver jets together swing and sweep around the sky. Like fish, like meteors, like falcons shooting. (A decrescendo of bowstrings plucked and they are past. . . . Now coming again. . . .) Tower, and jets swinging around it, you could hardly say which is lovelier. The tower is defective art. The jets are closer to nature, purer, like dewdrops on the grass, like fish, like wasps. But they are evanescent, lacking the stability of the unbalanced tower. In a moment they are gone, but the tower remains.

In the cathedral below, Galileo, seeing the great lantern swing at the end of its chain, discovered the principle of the pendulum. The same harmony is in the jets. (Was in the jets.)

✧

Our friends in Geneva are surprised that we have returned alive and whole after traveling over half Italy on a scooter. But they are no more surprised than I am. I live in the expectation of disaster. The passage of days, weeks, even years without it seems to me miraculous. I am full of gratitude.

Somewhere Montaigne says that his religious impulses are nourished by good fortune but weaken in adversity. He prays best when things go well. This is my case too. It seems to me that I lack adequate endowments for successful survival in this treacherous world. Yet I survive and, beyond all reason, prosper. Disaster snoops around me, sometimes crouches for the final spring. But always there is the unexpectable coincidence, a letter in the mail, an encounter in the street. . . . Disaster snoops away again. It seems to me that my case is the opposite of Job's in the Old Testament. I cannot believe that I do not owe a debt of gratitude somewhere. I thank God.

Is this what we call Faith? I, a creature committed to rationality, will not have it so. Faith is no virtue. Why should anyone be proud of holding a belief in the absence of evidence, or in spite of it? If I made up my mind to have Faith that the cosmos was ruled by a Barbary Ape would that be to my credit? Is it more to my credit if I have Faith in something more attractive?

It seems to me that only one question is relevant to belief: is this actually so? But when you believe something because you think you ought to, because it seems virtuous to believe it, or because it makes a comfortable belief, then you disqualify yourself for judgment, which must be critical. On that basis you may believe that the stars are diamonds (an unpoetic conception, not nearly as good as the truth). You may even believe that a sufficiently determined faith will make the untrue true, will change the stars to diamonds. This is vanity.

One of the cardinal virtues is humility. We should not claim that we are privy to God's thought, that we are informed of his intentions and can tell the rest of the world about them, that the architecture of the

cosmos has been made known to us. It is rare that it is
not sinful to be a preacher.

✤

Our common morality stands most easily on its
head. The Pharisee who identified himself with virtue
on the street-corners was denounced as a sinner by
Christ; but it is he whom we account moral. We revere
the man who presumes to speak for God and are
shocked by the man of no faith, the agnostic, the one
who says he does not know.

I like the oracle who found Socrates the wisest man
in the world because he knew his own ignorance. It
has not been given us to apprehend ultimate realities.
The best thing is to acknowledge this, where we don't
know to say we don't know.

But this can be dangerous. We go by easy steps
from: *Socrates does not know anything about God* to
Socrates does not believe in God to *Socrates denies
God*. Yet it is evident now, when all passions have
been spent, that Socrates was moved by a sense of
divinity more than the mass of his fellow citizens who
had Faith.

Perhaps, if the hemlock had been handed to the
right parties, Athens would have been depopulated.

Belief should not have to be absolute. Why can I
not say (since it is the case) that I do not know
whether there is such a being as God, but I think
there is something of the sort, or I feel intimations of
such a power?

Experience has taught me to be grateful when
things go well, though this may be vanity. Experience
has made me feel that I must try to be worthy of good
fortune, that while the unknown power seems to be
understanding and forgiving (in my case), my own
deserving must still be looked to. But I have no way
of knowing whether this has any meaning in theologi-
cal terms. I act on the best intimations which experi-

ence has furnished me, and take comfort in them,
without certain knowledge of what they represent.

If I should hear voices such as came to Joan of
Arc, if God should appear to me as he did to Moses,
still I could not be sure, in the absolute sense, that the
experience was not a hallucination. It reaches me
through channels I cannot trust. Though moved by
religious experience, I would still be an agnostic.

We should not close our eyes to reality in order to
enjoy visions.

Meanwhile, I am grateful that we are back alive and
whole.

✧

I don't understand how Mrs. Calvin's son John knew
for sure the basis on which God separates the saved
from the damned (he not having interviewed God or
been in the afterworld himself yet).

Speaking of boundaries. . . . If mankind inhabited a
land bounded by a mountain-range beyond which no
one had ever seen, there still would be men to describe
the landscape on the other side. And we would believe
them rather than bear the burden of recognized
ignorance.

✧

The Water Rail, I find, is still in Geneva. The lake is
lower than ever and the rail would have more mud to
pick at, except that now he cannot bring himself to
leave the reeds at all. I see him only in glimpses
through their margin, still stalking and picking, head
down. He has no great thoughts. He will die, someday,
and perhaps that same Johnny Calvin will not admit
him to the afterworld.

✧

Many persons who profess a religion, I suspect, do
not believe absolutely. But they are conscious of re-

ligious experience as I am. Each cultivates the experience in his own way, which is not necessarily my way. To many this means going to church every Sunday, professing an absolute creed out loud, singing hymns known from childhood, listening to the lofty rhetoric of a sermon. Most want a congregation with which to share the experience; other voices added to their own, all around them, participating in a common ritual, supporting them. (For myself, I would sooner look to find God in the deserted church.)

Some count beads, some say set prayers. A distinguished flutist from whom I take weekly lessons (as another man goes to church) told me that the performance of flute exercises is like prayer to him. *"C'est une religion."* (The man who repeats his *Pater Noster* daily may not be taking the words literally. He is doing his flute exercises.)

I don't see how you could separate the expression of any art from something like divine grace. The classification of musical compositions as either religious or secular, sacred or profane, is a mere convenience. All true music is religious, Bach's secular cantatas no less than his church cantatas. The paintings of Pieter Breughel are as sacred as those of Fra Angelico. What is profane is not art.

❖

We now have a second Nightingale, for when the first breaks down.

The morning of April 26 my initial words were, "A Nightingale!" "What?" said B, between sleep and wake. Then she, too, listened.

That was the beginning of a performance which has not stopped since. The Nightingale has stationed himself in a hedgerow thirty feet from our bedroom window. He must nap a bit during the middle of the day and briefly at dusk. When at last it is full dark, however, with light only from the stars (and from the

Arand-Roland comet now hanging—head down, tail up—in our northern skies), he begins to sing and, according to our best observation, sings all night steadily. Not ever stopping; hardly ever pausing. At dawn the Blackbirds wake up and join him—or vie with him. Soon Blackcaps and others make a chorus. But as the sun mounts the chorus falls off and only our Nightingale's song continues steadily, unexhausted.

When does he sleep? How long can this keep up?

I could better understand the Chiffchaff repeating his *chiff chaff chiff* . . . all day and all night. But the Nightingale's song is energy and imagination disciplined by art. It is composition. It is a new creation in every passage, looking to improvement like a religious man practicing the flute. There is dedication in it. The concentration of the artist. (Perhaps he sings at night because that is the only time he has the air-waves to himself.)

If you do not see the bird you think the brilliant passages-at-music are separated by breathing pauses. But bill and throat are vibrating in these pauses, more and more, and you may hear a faint high Starling-note develop progressively. In an instant, now, out comes a repeated bead of music growing deeper and richer . . . till the series is cut off by a flourish.

Full stop.

Is he breathing now? No. Bill and throat are moving again with the note at first inaudible, now breaking into a different bead of music, or paired beads, repeated, developing, and cut off by a different flourish.

Lyly's *jug jug jug jug terheu* is the bare bones of the matter, the skeleton which is clothed with different flesh at each performance.

All possible tones are available, high and low, harsh, reedy, smooth, piercing. Challenging or fainting. Often cacks and clicks. To one who knows the Mockingbird this is equaled, and the Yellow-breasted Chat also astonishes this way. What is unequaled is the phrasing; the combination of rhythm and nuance; the rapid repetition, but with a development, a crescendo or a deepening of tone or a lifting, all proceeding rapidly (or sometimes slowly), then culminating in a terminal flourish of grace notes. Period. Begin again with a new motif, new nuance, new development, all over again, swell out . . . and stop abruptly with a new flourish. Invent endlessly, never quite repeating yourself.

No rule of composition is invariable. Sometimes the motif is repeated for ever, no flourish coming to end it. Time passes and it continues. How long . . . ? There! He is off on a new passage.

But in music the ear is as essential as the voice, and it is exhaustible. The taste of food depends on the state of my digestion. The taste of music too. When I have made a meal of Nightingale song, when I am surfeited, I find no attraction in it. It does not seem particularly musical. Let a few hours pass, however, and then the burst of song is like the Gates of Heaven opening. Angels' harps. Nothing that ever was written about the Nightingale does justice to this.

It is the same with Bach. With Botticelli. Or with Shakespeare.

Sometimes one prays the song will stop.

The time comes when what really arouses you is a true silence, as it did B and me one night. Full dark and nothing heard. We speculate. (There are cats about.) No, I say, it could not have gone on forever. He has played himself out. The song is exhausted, the rumpled singer a bundle of feathers lying somewhere on his back, bill open but forever silent.

Then, out of this silent dark, a flourish of notes like summer lightning, broken off as soon as begun. The silence still. Were we wrong? Almost a minute passes. Then the deepening note rising out of silence (like Venus from the sea), repeated, repeated—but the series left unfinished. Soon another start. In two minutes he is singing full, as he will all night, as he will still after

the sun rises. We stop listening, and the sound makes
a silence that is no longer strange.

(It is just as well, however, to have a spare Nightingale.)   ✧

On May Day we were awakened by the first Cuckoo
of the year. It was 5,768 o'clock.

To the native, the clock imitates the bird. To the
visitor from overseas it is the other way around.

Because King Richard II grew a companion to the
common streets, because he was daily swallowed by
men's eyes, so, when he had occasion to be seen he
was but as the Cuckoo is in June, heard, not regarded.
Let this be a lesson to the Cuckoo!

✧

In the Kingdom of Heaven all cities straddle rivers
(since they must have bridges), like Geneva. Like
Geneva, they all stand at the ends of lakes. All cities
are the size of Geneva (pop. 160,000). All have, as
their center, a hill with a church on top. All are en-
vironed by plains and mountains. All have Geneva's
weather, including the black *bise*.

The north wind rises with force, sweeping whitecaps along the lake and sending waves up on shore.
In no time a wizard's black invests the atmosphere. The
landscape is obscured by a smokiness, your view is
veiled. Sky heavy overhead, threatening rain which
does not come—never comes. But every day it gets
colder, and more of an ordeal to cross the Pont du
Mont-Blanc, which gets the *bise* full in the flank. . . .

Then you notice one evening that the *bise* is moder-
ating. Fewer whitecaps. At dusk the sky clears. All the
wizard's black vanishes, leaving an interim radiance
before the crystal darkness of night. Next day the sun
rises brilliantly in a clear sky. Everything is blue and
white and windy. You still have the *bise*, but no longer
a black *bise*, and in a few days it will have blown itself
out.   ✧

"The *bise* in the trees makes the birds sneeze," says Julie.

I have some mighty foolish children.

For example, it is of the utmost importance to them to keep track of the lake steamers. Mark announces at lunch that the *Général Dufour*, the *Savoie*, the *Valais*, and the *Montreux* were in port this morning. (But the *Vevey* was missing.) Smoke was trickling from the *Montreux*'s stack. (This makes everyone gratified and expectant.)

Later there is a shout: "A lake steamer!" Everyone rushes to see. There she is proceeding majestically up the lake, sparkling in the sunshine, a bone in her teeth. Which is she? Which is she?

I rush to the study for my binoculars (while everyone speculates and argues), rush out on the porch with them to look at the gold letters on the paddlewheel housing. "It *is* the *Montreux*!" Wild excitement. (Everybody: "It *is* it *is* the *Montreux*!") Now contentment settles on the household. We are fulfilled. . . .

Such childishness, after all! It makes no difference what boat it is. There is no reason for interrupting lunch, for everyone leaping from their seats, just because a lake steamer goes by. (With me it is the scientific impulse. Just as I must know what species of bird that is on our beach, so I must know which steamer. It is the business of science to put names to things.)

We simply cannot have this perpetual disorder. The children are utterly undisciplined. Nothing to do but bark at them. "Get back to the table, everyone!" I shout.

Mrs. Calvin's boy John, I am sure, never occupied his mind with the names of boats.

(Has anyone seen the *Vevey*?)

What I started to say was . . . I was going to remark
how essential it was that the Kingdom of Heaven have
irregular and unpredictable alternations of heavenly
and hellish weather. Otherwise the heavenly weather
would be but as the Cuckoo is in June. . . .

Moreover, bad weather is good. It satisfies the
ascetic in me. (The gods can see that I don't have it all
easy.) Let the wind and the rain strike, let the heating
system break down. (This is better than drowsing in
the tropics.) Not for too long, though.

I cannot tell where, but somewhere on its way from
Geneva to the Camargue the *bise* becomes no longer
the *bise*. The poetry of Provence infects its identity and
it becomes the *mistral*.

Between the water and the mud is soup of mud
through which birds wade. It flows about their moving
bodies, caressing them, feeling them secretly below the
Plimsoll line. The great white swans, when they ex-
change shore for water or water for shore, have to pay
this tribute. They move through the soup in a succession of breast-pushing heaves, stately still in their
shame.

The Garganey, I am sorry to say, like it. Too dainty
for dust (one would say they were), the products of
some celestial silversmith. They ought to keep themselves under glass. But they love to taste mud, to im-
merse bodies and bills into it up to the eyes, pushing
through it slowly to plough a furrow that closes behind
them. But they remain delicate in the midst of indeli-
cacy, and emerge unsullied.

"I have ploughed the sea," said Bolívar as he lay on
his death-bed, the victim of Original Sin.[1] These dainty

---

[1] See *Genesis* 2:17 and 3:19.

teal, these stately swans—they too must pay the price of Original Sin. They are one with Bolívar, one with John Calvin, Doctor of Jurisprudence. They too know concupiscence and death; they too are born of the mud, into the mud to descend.

❖

For a week on our shoreline the companion in sin of the Garganey has been a Bar-tailed Godwit. But his legs are not the mud-pedals which were attached to the bodies of swans and teal as afterthoughts.

His body and these stalks are parts of one design. The body is merely a place for the wings to fold into when he comes to rest, and that is why it is leaf-shaped. It also serves as a mount for the probe or swizzle-stick which he keeps immersed in the lovely mud, moving it back and forth, treading like a dancer as he goes.

In a week of constant close association with the Garganey (never more than inches away in feeding, often enclosed by them) he has become one of them. When I go down to the shore all lift their heads out of the mud, becoming alert and suspicious (or perhaps respectful). The Garganey edge out into the water, away from the embrace of the mud, ready to take off. The godwit remains a moment where he is. Then one teal rises fluttering and all are off, springing into the air, light-bodied like sandpipers now (not like ducks in mud). They sweep and scatter on the wind, this way and that, here and away and here again, adazzle in the sunlight, winkling like flashing mirrors, like gossamer adorned with spangles in the wind. The godwit can't be left behind, mustn't be left behind! Off he goes, legs now accessory and trailing. (Wait for me!) Off he goes, flicking his wings with the joy of being a teal, one of the sparklers himself like any other.

But now the flock, flung out from shore, half divides and half divides again, some this way, some that. Here or there they fall down, poise, drop onto the surface—

some, finally all. No spangles left in the sky, now, just little companies of silver Garganey floating on silver water. Placid. But what is this? One of the company is up still, flying and poising over the little groups, over one after another, back and forth. What is this? Still flying when the signal was to put down! An outcast. Maladjusted. No more a Garganey among his boon fellows, but a godwit alone in the big universe.

What I have been meaning to write about is the Water Rail, not Bolívar and the godwit. But the Water Rail has not been faithful to me lately. I hardly ever see him any more. Perhaps he has found another writer. After all—he is he and I am I. (I could pick at the mud if I wanted to, or swim for that matter, but he can't write.)

✧

The edge of a wheat field in the north of France is not the worst place to wake up. When I began to awaken I found myself on my feet, facing a man who was asking me a question in French. It was a bright hot day. The man was asking whether he could take us in his truck to Amiens. This was a puzzle. Why should anyone want to take us (whoever us was) in a truck to Amiens? To gain time I asked: Where is Amiens? He said it was only fifteen kilometers. By a mental effort then, as when one tries to wake up from a dream, I remembered that we were living in Geneva, in Europe. I asked Johnny, who turned out to be standing by, where we had been.

He said Beauvais.

As in a dream it began to come back to me about visiting Beauvais. At my feet I saw the scooter, its front end crumpled.

"I remember myself of nothing," I said to the man.

"It is the sun," he said sympathetically. "It is only the effect of the sun."

John said, in English: "I'll be able to explain to him in a minute. I'm still too scared to be able to say it in French." (He didn't seem scared.)

I asked him if he was hurt. He showed me a faint scratch on one leg, as if he regretted having nothing better to show. (But he was glad of at least this.) I made a more fitting appearance. Then did I "wear a garment all of blood and stain my favours in a bloody mask."

It began to come back to me, then, leaving Paris, scooting to Beauvais, planning to visit Amiens, then to join B and the other children, who were traveling by car direct from Geneva, at Saint Quentin. (John confirmed that it was Saint Quentin.) I had a dream of the scooter suddenly in a field full of little ditches, not being able to control it.

We would be appreciative if you could conduct us to Amiens, I told the kind man. Is there not a train from there to Saint Quentin?

He said indeed there would be!—his voice full of solicitude. I told him that John was too scared to speak French.

What he needs, he said, is a drink.

I said that what I needed was to wash my face.

There is a place where we shall do both on the way, he said.

Another man with a bicycle was there, and together they lifted the great mangled scooter into the truck (a plumbing-supply truck).

Away we went now, the long fields of wheat, the big shade trees (elms) and spots of woodland, as lovely in the white heat and shimmering sunlight as I remembered them on the scooter before the moment that divides the past from the future. I felt sad.

Perhaps we will have time to visit the cathedral before the train, I told Johnny, trying to retrieve the day. But we didn't. Our rescuer, having lifted a glass to John's juice of orange and my vermouth in a village café (where I washed my face, returning to the past), drove us on to the station in Amiens, helped ship the scooter to Boulogne, helped ship ourselves to Saint-Quentin, and gave me a brother's farewell (to John an uncle's farewell).

I wish I had asked his name, at least to have written him later. He disappeared, and he is lost forever. And so I am lost too, and John with me.

✧

"Do you have a clear purpose in life?" I asked Tessa, who had joined our household in England and made herself one of our children.

It was clear that she had not, and was troubled only at the thought that I might expect her to have one. She rolled over on her back, paws in air, and wagged her whole body in atonement.

Writing from England in 1915, Dr. L. P. Jacks said: "I believe that twelve months of war have brought to England a peace of mind such as she has not possessed for generations. . . . It is nothing more or less than the peace of mind which comes to every man who, after tossing about among uncertainties and trying his hand at this and that, finds at last a mission, a cause to which he can devote himself body and soul. At last he has something to live for. . . ."

Writing from England in 1915, Graham Wallas said: "A state of consciousness must be judged not only by its momentary quality, but by its continuance, and 'the peacefulness of being at war' is doomed by the nature of things to be transitory. If the world-war were to last in its present intensity for a whole generation, it would become a conflict of famished women and children fighting each other with their teeth and nails. . . . I know that there are men in Germany who are in like case with myself. . . . Should any one of them read this, I send him greeting, and assure him of my conviction that if ever that imperfect community of nations is to be reconstituted, of which England and Germany once formed part, there will be work for those who during the war have denied themselves the luxury of mental peace."[2]

Tessa had got to her feet, all alertness to her ear-tips. "Shall I fetch whatever it is?" she was plainly asking.

"Better let me think about it first," I said.

❖

The German tourists—lovely, young, fresh, and chattering—look at the bombed-out sites around St. Paul's in London as at moon-craters. The English tourists in Frankfurt look at the bombed-out sites as the German tourists in London look at the bombed-out sites—lovely, young, fresh, and chattering.

❖

I have said that we have a Water Rail at our place in Geneva. But it is not always the same Water Rail. Several times, for example, I have seen it twice at the same time, following itself about, or emerging from the reeds to cross its own path while it was still in full view and disappear into the reeds again while it remained in view of the path it had just crossed behind itself and disappeared. I have seen it chase itself—or maybe being chased by itself.

Finally, as a result of there being two of itself it has become three. But the third and newest is not it at all. At least, not yet. It is much smaller, a pompon of black velvet with a white point on it that I think is bill, and with much-too-long legs with which it scampers (when it ought to toddle).

But I shall get back to the Water Rail. . . .

[2] Both quotations are from *The New Republic*, September 11, 1915.

Men sometimes await indefinitely what has already happened. ("I tell you that Elijah has already come, and they did not know him. . . .")

In the middle of the night I awoke to the voice of the Nightingale again, uttered with authority from the tangle of shrubbery under our window, and now for the first time I knew whose voice it was.

✧

I wish to say a word for the Wheatear. . . .

WHITE-WINGED BLACK TERNS   BLACK TERNS

THE majority of the world's terns are seabirds of the seacoasts, belonging to the familiar genus *Sterna* or closely similar genera. Distinguished from this majority by habit and habitat alike are the three species of *Chlidonias*, which we identify in the vernacular as "marsh terns." They are the Black Tern, the White-winged Black Tern, and the Whiskered Tern. These three form a group so distinct that in French they are called, not by the word for tern ("sterne"), but by a generic name of their own, "guifettes."

The Black Tern, which is the only marsh tern found in the New World, is the only common one in most of Europe. Of the other two, the white-wing nests chiefly in Asia with an extension of its range into eastern Europe, while the Whiskered Tern nests in southern Europe, in the Middle East, in the warmer parts of Asia, in southeast Africa, Australia, and New Zealand.

Unlike other terns, these three breed in fresh-water marshes, where they build floating nests attached to the marsh vegetation. Another distinction is that, instead of plunging from the air to catch small fish beneath the surface of the water, they live largely on insects which they normally pick from the surface in flight, although they also hawk for them like swallows.

Here in Geneva, at the end of Lac Léman where it empties into the Rhône, the migrating Black Terns pass through in April, May, and June, presumably coming up the long river from the Mediterranean and, after leaving the lake, crossing the Swiss plateau to the upper Rhine. In August and September, now mostly in their winter plumage, they pass through again on their return to Africa. We scrutinize the transient flocks spring and fall for the occasional representatives of one of the other two species that we may find among them. In the case of the white-wings, which share common wintering grounds with the Black Terns in Africa, one supposes that individuals caught up in their flocks on spring migration are thereby drawn away from their proper migration-routes, and that this accounts for the appearance of a few in central and western Europe every spring.

Since I am, myself, as aquatic in my habits as a busy city-dweller can be, I have better opportunities than most to observe the flocks of Black Terns as they transit Geneva. From my home to my office on the other side of the lake is some two and a half miles, which I traverse in my motor-boat, the *Snark II*, often four times a day. I sometimes spend a morning or afternoon adrift and working in the middle of the lake, more accessible to grebes, ducks, gulls, and terns than to people.

The morning of May 8, 1967 the lake was swarming with Black Terns. They were so widely scattered over an indefinite area that the best I could do was to estimate, as my notes have it, "a thousand or thousands" in the parts of the lake that fell under my observation. In addition, there were five Whiskered Terns perched on the stakes and wires of an offshore fence that bounds a marshy nature-preserve adjacent to my home.

For the next ten days I spent as much time as I could on the lake, writing and observing the terns at the same time. Since the terns showed no fear of the *Snark*, whether moving or still, but would come within inches of it, I often had them swarming about me when I was simply drifting out in the lake. At other times I traveled in the midst of the flocks, maintaining the same speed, as they flew and fed just over the surface on either side. After ten days of this I felt a certain intimacy with them, and some familiarity with their behavior.

My intimacy was not only with the Black Terns. Scattered among them, day after day, were White-winged Black Terns, of which I once saw as many as ten at a time. There were Whiskered Terns too; but when they were in any numbers they tended to band together, apart from the others, and for three days there was a flock of thirteen along the east shore of the lake that was not associated with the other terns at all. Little Gulls, which resemble the marsh terns in size and manner of feeding, were also present on occasional days. So far inland, these smallest of gulls are uncommon migrants, and one flock of fifteen was by far the largest I had seen in my ten years on the lake. However, although they sometimes flew and fed briefly with the terns, they preferred to associate with their own congeners, the few non-breeding Black-headed Gulls that remain with us during the breeding season.

The Black Tern in its spring plumage has an all-black body and head, somber gray mantle and tail, pale under-wings, and white undertail coverts that flash as the bird tilts in its flight. The White-winged Black Tern, indistinguishable from it except by its markings and voice, also has a black body and head; but it is black under the wings as well, while the upper wing coverts and the whole of the tail are white. This is a spectacular reversal of the rule that birds are light below and dark above. On the other hand, the Whiskered Tern has the essential pattern of the typical *Sternas*, except that it is darker on the upper surfaces of wings

and tail, and gray on the underside of its body. This body-gray is separated from its black cap by a narrow white zone on either side, which constitutes the "moustache" that gives the species its name ("guifette moustac" in French). The Whiskered Tern is also somewhat larger and, consequently, not as quick in aerial maneuver as the other two. It might plausibly be regarded as intermediate between them and the typical terns, which accounts for its having been given the specific name *hybrida*. However, the generic identity of all three, distinguishing them from other terns, is more evident when they put on their winter plumages, in which it is hard to tell them apart.

I know of no bird more deft and delicate in its flight, more dainty in its feeding on the wing, than the Black Tern and white-wing. I lump the two in this because, not only were they indistinguishable to me in form, flight, and behavior, they themselves appeared to make no distinction in their association. Unlike the Whiskered Terns, the white-wings, even when there were several of them, tended to be scattered as individuals among the blacks. Consequently, what I say here about flight and behavior applies to black and white-wing alike, but not necessarily to the somewhat heavier Whiskered Tern.

When the lake is flat calm and the birds are moving in straightaway flight just over its surface, each will continually lift and drop again in a little undulation, as if rising over an invisible obstacle. A more formal maneuver, not performed so close to the surface, is almost identical with the trick of the Wood Pigeon in its courtship flight, familiar to all observers in the parks and gardens of Europe. The bird suddenly sets its wings, bent downward, and in that rigid position rises over an imaginary hump and glides down again on the other side, thereupon resuming its normal flight. All three species engage in this. When not feeding but intent on going somewhere, these birds fly not unlike typical terns, with a long galloping wing-stride the power of which is seen in the successive impulses given by each beat. At other times, when they fly close to the surface, the wing-motion is more rapid and irregular. The wings beat faster for a moment as the bird veers, or there is a slight backing of the wings for a pause in flight. The bird tilts, swerves, hesitates, advances, master of the invisible medium, every movement in perfect poise. Its flight is an allegro with turns and grace-notes.

On calm spring days the lake is seen to be covered by minute midges or midgelike insects resting on the surface. The terns in their passage take each one by a single flick of the bill, down and up again. When the waves are running, however, they cannot keep so close to the surface, and then they have to dip down each time to pick off their prey; but they do it with the same flick of the bill.

The Black Terns and white-wings are not only sociable but appear to take a delight in flocking as densely as possible. They feed in loosely scattered companies over the surface, but suddenly are seized by a common impulse that draws them together in one tight band—like dancing gnats, or like small shorebirds. The band then rises high in the air, sweeps away and back again in this direction and that, a small cloud of birds constantly changing its shape. After two or three minutes of such evolutions it disperses again as suddenly, its members scattering over the surface to resume their feeding. Often, when they have moved far enough up-wind in their feeding, they flock like this to return to where they began.

Scattered, the birds are relatively silent, with only an occasional cry, but when they suddenly draw together their cries multiply. Part of the impression of joy in their close association comes from this utterance. The flocks appear to be vocal in proportion to their density. The cries of the Black Terns were a variety of musical cheeps. On the one or two occasions when I heard the white-wing among them the note was equally musical but lower pitched and with a roll in it. The Whiskered Terns that I heard had an unmusical cry, closer to those of the *Sterna* species.

Even though they have webbed feet, terns differ from gulls in that they do not rest and swim on the water. When they alight it is always on a bit of driftwood, a buoy, or a post. But there are exceptions, and one of the occasional flock exercises of the terns I lived with for ten days was to assemble on the surface, all crying, so close as virtually to touch one another flank-to-flank. The individual birds seemed unstable, their heads high, their long wing-points and tails sticking up, so that one might have expected a breath of air to capsize them. And they never rested tranquilly on the water. For the most part they bathed, splashed, and preened. Individuals were always taking off, almost vertically, or coming to a splash-down abruptly among the others. Frequently the whole flock would sweep off, as if blown away by a puff of wind, only to return and drop back at precisely the same spot, all playing together on the surface again.

Finally, in the manner of the flocks of Black-headed Gulls, a flock of these terns on the wing would suddenly be taken with a frenzy in which each individual plunged, zoomed, and swerved among all the others, just avoiding collisions as they shot past one another.

I have no means of knowing whether the birds I saw day after day were the same individuals or new arrivals replacing others that had continued their migration. The problem was to know what became of them at night. In my limited observation of the marsh terns, they like to find roosting points, such as floating driftwood and stakes, where they have water around and beneath them; but there are hardly enough such roosts available near Geneva for the numbers that were present during these days. Everything indicated that they did not pass their nights roosting on the local piers and breakwaters, but left the vicinity of Geneva altogether.

On May 10 after sunset, my son Mark and I went out in the *Snark* to watch. As dusk fell, successive contingents of terns, drawing together in the usual tight and vociferous flocks, circled up into the fading sky until at last they could no longer be seen except through my nine-power binoculars, and through them only as specks. At that height they formed several broad, straggling U's and moved off steadily northward, as if on parade, until they were gone. One last contingent of about a hundred continued to feed over the surface, but finally flew off northward too, we following below. It rose higher and higher until it had disappeared in the gathering dusk.

This behavior suggested nocturnal migration. But the lake extends north from Geneva, although bending east after some miles, so that the flocks might have been on their way to roosting sites farther up it. The height to which all but the last contingent rose, however, suggested that they were going far, and after the first fifteen miles, in the direction they were taking, they would have left the lake completely. Gulls going up the lake from Geneva often fly northeastward, cutting overland to join it again above its bend. But as the terns were heading at dusk they would soon be north of it and, if they continued in the same direction, past the lakes of Neuchâtel and Bienne, they would at last reach the Rhine in the vicinity of Basel, some 130 miles from Geneva as the tern flies.

The evening of the 11th we again went out in the *Snark* to see what would happen. Again at dusk the terns circled upward in dense flocks that then made

off northward, this time before reaching such a height
as the flocks of the evening before. We followed below
as far as we could, but soon lost them.

Although I had been allowed to live among these
terns throughout every day, every evening at dusk,
like creatures in a fairy-tale, they departed for the
unknown, leaving the earthbound behind to wonder
and to remember.

SCENE: GENEVA

TIME: A MORNING IN JUNE

In June 1961 negotiations were going on in the French town of Évian, on the south shore of the Lake of Geneva, between a delegation of the French Government headed by M. Louis Joxe, and representatives of the Algerian rebellion against French rule, namely Messrs. Krim Belkacem, Ahmed Francis, Mohammed Ben Yahia, Ahmed Boumendjel, and Redha Malek. Because the Algerian delegation refused to be lodged on French soil, although agreeing to negotiate on it, accommodations were provided for it by the Swiss Government in neutral Geneva, together with daily transportation by two helicopters between that city and Évian. The principal issue of the negotiations, which were to eventuate in Algerian independence, was whether the Sahara Desert should belong to France or Algeria. General de Gaulle was President of France. General Challe was one of the leaders of the revolt against President de Gaulle's Government that had been mounted in Algeria by French Army officers the previous April. Upon its failure he had been tried and, on May 31, sentenced to fifteen years in prison.

Also in June 1961, a major international conference to end the civil war in Laos was going on in Geneva, as was a conference of the members of the General Agreement on Tariffs and Trade (GATT). Mr. Averell Harriman was the American representative at the conference on Laos. Mr. Arthur Dean, Mr. Feodor Tsarapkin, and Sir Michael Wright, representing the United States, Russia, and Britain respectively, were at the same time negotiating in Geneva for the discontinuance of nuclear weapons tests.

The swans, Coots, kites, and Swifts that resided on the lake, ignorant of our political boundaries and disputes (they have their own boundaries and disputes in June), had no part in all these negotiations; but it was not sure that in a world of nuclear armaments they would not be affected by their outcome.

The following article appeared in The New Republic *of June 19, 1961.*

IN GENEVA the laborer's day begins at seven o'clock. Businessmen and shop-keepers are on the job by eight. The diplomatic world moves more ponderously: international conferences don't get under way before ten.

The Professor, whose mind bears the burden of the Higher Knowledge (plus, if the truth were known, some Middle High Nonsense as well), makes a nobler beginning. At five minutes to eight his wife has at last driven off from the front door, carrying the disorderly pack of children away with her to school. This is the quiet hour when he says his matins on the flute.

At a quarter to nine he bethinks him at last of the day's work—for which the day will, as always, be too short. He puts away his flute and dials 162 to get the weather report. A center of high pressure (he is told) has appeared over the Azores and will influence the time in our country from tomorrow; for the present, however, the time will rest unstable.

Out of the house he goes, then, brief-case in hand, descending the grassy slope to the lakeshore. Heavy clouds, like water-colors still wet on the paper, hang low on the opposite shore, threatening to break and run down over the landscape.

Far up the lake toward Lausanne, however, the sky has opened out, its blue framed by the stormy darkness closer in. The land up that way is bathed in misty morning radiance from some spotlight hidden behind the proscenium.

The Professor steps off the pier into the waiting *Snark* (which bobs down and up in response to his footfall) and casts her off with accustomed movements. He pulls the cord of the outboard motor, which clears its throat, coughs, then settles down to a steady low roaring. The swan with her four downy young (hatched three days ago) sails up to the gunwale to beg bread and then, just as a precaution, hisses at the Professor. The *Snark* moves forward at first slowly under the Professor's masterly guidance, then springs to life and dashes out into the lake, taking the dabbling Coot by surprise. They had not expected her to be upon them so soon. Now they are forced to scatter with running steps over the water, at last taking flight.

The *Snark*, her whole bow lifted out of the lake now, runs over the wavelets with a pattering sound like that made by the flying feet of the Coot on the water. Farther out, the lake is covered with Swifts, veering and swerving all about, sometimes so close across the *Snark's* bow that only their agility saves them. A Black Kite—talons hanging, wings half folded—comes tumbling down from the dark clouds like a torn cloth kite out of control. It brushes the surface of the lake near the rocketing *Snark* and lifts itself up again, once more in control, now heavily beating its wings.

Across the lake the *Palais des Nations* is a small architectural blot on the landscape, looking naked. From somewhere to the left of it, two great birds have just risen above the land, against the background of cloud. No—by their manner of flight not birds. The Professor identifies them as belonging to the Order *Helicoptera* of the Class *Insecta*. Looking at his wristwatch, he notes that it is already five past nine.

Even for the diplomatic world the day's work is beginning. The two helicopters come bumbling across the lake, passing over the *Snark* as it parts the waters beneath them. They bear the Algerian delegation from its nocturnal roost in Switzerland to the site of the Peace Conference with the French Government at Évian, on the French side of the lake. Below are the

Professor and the *Snark*, cutting their furrow through the lapping waters, throwing their bow-wave carelessly off to either side, leaving their long, bubbly, disappearing wake for the rebel chieftains to admire. Above are the chieftains themselves: Belkacem, Francis, Ben Yahia, Boumendjel, and Malek. Peace be to them, and to M. Louis Joxe, and to Generals de Gaulle and Challe, and to all mankind this fine (but uncertain) spring morning!

As the helicopters dwindle toward the opening beyond the dark proscenium, the Professor brings the *Snark* heeling over in a snaky curve—then, throttling down, into the walled enclosure of the Port Barton. He moors her, picks up his brief-case, gets out and walks up the path toward the main building of the Graduate Institute of International Studies. In the trees above him the Wood Pigeons coo peace.

Upstairs in his office, he looks out the window, up the lake toward the blue sky. The helicopters must be landing at Évian now, in sunlight. M. Louis Joxe (who roosts with his French delegation at Évian) has had his cup of coffee, perhaps also a croissant with jam, and is on his way to the conference-site to meet with the Algerian chiefs. French soldiers with tommy-guns stand at attention as he passes.

At various points in Geneva, by now, the chattering and smiling Chinese Communists, the relaxed British, a peculiar assortment of Laotians, Mr. Averell Harriman, and some heavy-set Russians are getting into their respective limousines to be driven to the *Palais des Nations*, where they will sit around a table to determine whether Laotians, Cambodians, and perhaps all the rest of us as well (including swans hatched only three days ago) are to live or die. Peace be to them too!

Just off the Rue de Lausanne the delegates to the GATT Conference will be meeting in a few minutes to decide whether the GATT is loaded. Peace to their souls too!

In a nearby room Mr. Arthur Dean, Mr. Feodor Tsarapkin, and Sir Michael Wright will be talking about nuclear tests—deciding, perhaps, whether the Wood Pigeons shall breathe pure or irradiated air.

The Professor thinks about the Problem of the Sahara, worrying for a moment over the future of Algeria, Tunisia, Morocco, and all the rest of us (including the swans and the Swifts). He thinks about the Problem of Policing the Cease-fire in Laos, worrying for a moment over the future of Vietnam and all the rest of us (including the kites and the Coot). Then he remembers that a high-pressure area is approaching from the Azores, so that tomorrow ought to be sunny. With that he settles down happily to the day's work. . . . God bless us every one!

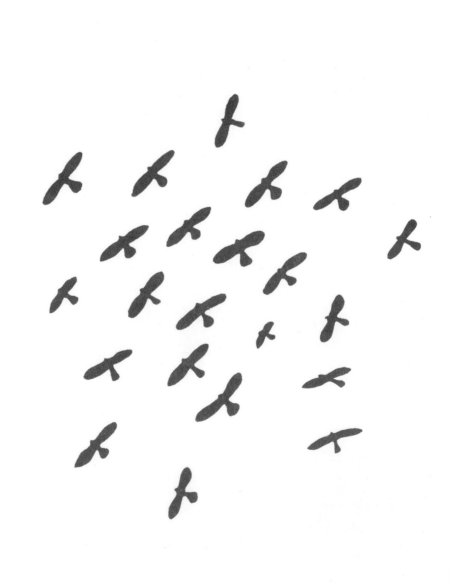

ALPINE CHOUGHS IN A VALLEY

THE common Crow in America and the Carrion Crow, its European counterpart, have not given the crow family a reputation for either gracefulness or musical ability. Ravens and Jackdaws, by contrast, are adept on the wing, but we know from Aesop how the Raven made a fool of himself when, at the fox's invitation, he opened his mouth to sing.

The Alpine Chough is a small crow with a yellow bill and red legs. Its home, summer and winter, is among the rock faces, crags, and towers of the high Alps, where snow lies the year around. Here it nests in crannies; here it roosts colonially in January as in August. It is sociable not only with its own kind, for in recent years it has taken increasingly to association with us people. Every morning in winter the colonies drop from their spires and steeples, sweep down many thousands of feet, many miles through snowy passes and intermontane valleys, arriving at last in selected villages or towns. Here all day they scatter among the roof-tops, over the balconies and ledges and window-sills, disporting themselves among the artificial cliffs and crags, accepting gracefully morsels of tribute offered by villagers, townsmen, and tourists at the resort-hotels. In the evening they allow the updrafts to lift them once more to their inaccessible homes. At sunset, as at sunrise, never a chough is to be found in the settlements.

The Alpine village of Les Granges, perched at three thousand feet above the upper Rhône Valley, enjoys their daily visitations throughout the nesting season. They come down for the cutting of the hay, to feed where the scythe has struck, and for the cherries. But when nesting is over and cherries gone they come no more, not even for a second haying. Try to find them now! All day, presumably, as well as all night, they are at their homes among the glaciers.

No bird is so buoyant on the wing. The Raven is strong, deft, and acrobatic; but the chough, surely, is lighter than air. It is not like a bird of great wing that bears against the air-currents with its weight and so is uplifted. Instead, it floats like a fish. It swims as if in a medium heavier than itself. It rises or falls, this way or that, with a twist of tail or wing. It sinks through the air a thousand feet to inspect some spot on the terrestrial surface, finds its answer, and as though released from gravity rises up again.

The choughs are always in loose flocks—twenty, thirty, forty, or a hundred—that swim through the gorges and valleys, and over the passes, like schools of fish. They are too buoyant to rest except on the wing, and though they touch ground frequently it is only to mount again. A school will drift around the shoulder of a hill, sweep this way and that, then all drop together to begin feeding in a field of newly cut hay— perhaps almost under the scythe of the farmer. But a moment later they lift up again, drift sideways, swing about, and come down, half of them in another field, half on roof-tops. They rise, even from flat ground, without beating their wings—simply letting go.

Wherever the choughs are one hears constantly their repeated musical call, a soft *kree* . . . , like crickets low-pitched and mellow. One would admire it even in a thrush. It keeps them together, I suppose, when cloud or blizzard envelops them.

Before the middle of August the choughs were no longer to be seen about Les Granges. Three thousand feet above, at a lake cradled by the summits of the Dents du Midi, one might still see half a dozen where scores had been. Then one saw them no more even there. It was understood that they had gone higher— but there was hardly room for them higher unless they roosted on clouds!

August 17 we were at the lake by midday. After lunch we set off up the stony slope where we have found Ptarmigan, where Wheatears and Water Pipits bob up on the rocks, where the marmots whistle from all sides (a whistling ground-squirrel is like a musical crow), to climb Le Luisin, which is over nine thousand feet high, then return to cross the Col d'Emeney into the remote Emeney Valley, where we had never been. The summit of Le Luisin is a rocky point in space, falling sharply away on all sides, facing across a void (earth is eight thousand feet below) toward the long range of Alps from Mont Blanc to the Matterhorn. A black flake rose rapidly from below, veered suddenly close in as if carried by a dangerous current, and touched down on the summit-rocks beside us. Then we saw other choughs back and below, toward the Emeney Valley.

Arriving at the top of the pass, after coming down from the summit, one looks into the head of a deep valley bounded by a buttressed stone wall several thousand feet high, its face broken where white streams pour from melting snows and fall vertically through space. Far below, where our trail leads, one can see the green of a meadow.

Here in the isolated grandeur of this great bowl are, surely, all the choughs in Switzerland! It is like find-

ing the Elephants' Graveyard. Hundreds of black flakes drift below us, at our level, above us, close to us and far away, constantly uttering their musical cry. Each bird moves individually within the movement of the whole, on its own business, skimming a grassy outcrop, touching the cliff here or there, sheering off again. A detachment from the main company, all creeking musically, lands among the crevices and cracks of cliffs just above us, some perching vertically like Swifts. At one moment all the birds are about us; the next they are at the opposite side of the valley, or a thousand feet below.

Winding along the slope, we go steeply down into the valley single file, descending as if from Shangri-la; then follow the valley toward its opening above a gorge. Now we are on familiar earth, in forest of larch and spruce where Crossbills adorn the spires and Nutcrackers sun themselves. We have emerged from the Valley of the Choughs into the real world again.

THE common belief used to be that species existed as such in nature, each having been formed as a distinct creation on that day when, according to *Genesis*, God created all the living creatures "according to their kinds." Difficulties arose, however, when it came to listing them. Upon close examination it might transpire that the members of what one had regarded as a single species were not, in fact, uniform. Those that lived in the desert, perhaps, were paler than those that lived in the woods. Did this mean that they constituted two species rather than one, that God or nature had in fact created two "kinds" where a cursory observation had previously revealed only one?

Again, the resemblances among species by virtue of which they tended to fall into groups (e.g., the dogs, the cats, the monkeys, etc.), was not explained by the theory that each had been separately created, without relationship to others. It suggested, rather, that God had created genera or families as well as species.

As soon as one attempted to list the "kinds" (as Linnaeus, for example, did in the eighteenth century) it became apparent that the situation was more complicated than the simple words of *Genesis* made it seem. If there were species, as everyone assumed, were there not subspecies and superspecies as well? Any list one made, then, would have to be a hierarchical list, based on a system of graduated classification.

The concept that the species had each been created separately gave way, in the nineteenth century, to the concept of their gradual emergence in the process of evolution. If there were distinct species in the present, they had not always been distinct. The species of the present had, rather, separated from one another in the long course of their descent from a common ancestor. Evolution presented the picture of a Tree of Life, branching and rebranching in time from a common stock.

This picture, by implication, destroyed the old concept of distinct species. A picture of branches diverging from a common stock, of differences that are at first imperceptible becoming greater over the generations, is the picture of a continuum in which everything is connected with everything else. Nature had not marked off graduated stages in this continuum, prescribing that, at this stage, the widening difference has become a difference of subspecies, at the next a difference of species, at the next a difference of genus. These categories, then, do not exist as such in nature any more than degrees Fahrenheit exist as such in nature. While warmer and colder do exist in nature, the stages that we mark off on our thermometers are merely nominal devices that help us describe what exists. It is essentially the same with species.

In the case of species, however, the artificiality of our categories tends to be hidden from us by the fact that we see the world only as it is at one moment in the progress of evolution—namely, our present. If our physical vision were not confined to this moment but included all the past as well, we would find ourselves unable to draw a line that separated, say, the Mallard (*Anas platyrhynchos*) from the Gadwall (*A. strepera*); for we would see back down both branches, of which they were merely the branch-ends, to the point at which they joined; we would see a spectrum of change, or a continuum, uniting the two ends in a perfect bond, making them one. In that case, we could not say that there were two species, *platyrhynchos* and *strepera*. We would have to say, rather, that there was a single range of continuous variation within the two extreme limits. And if we extended our vision further back in time, to more remote branchings in the Tree of Life, we could not even isolate what was between these extremes, for it in turn would be seen to merge imperceptibly with other branches. Nowhere would we find any lines of division, any sharp joints. We would have to conclude that all life was one.

We can best picture this situation if we will imagine a series of skins representing all the individual ancestors of the Common Loon, and another representing all the individual ancestors of the House Sparrow, both extending back to the point where they meet in a common ancestor; but all laid out in a straight line from the loon at one end to the sparrow at the other (in other words, the V branching from the common ancestor flattened out). Nowhere would we find any break in the perfect, imperceptible gradation from one end to the other. Nowhere would we find even such a division as would correspond to the forking of a branch—for, although the descendants of the common ancestor might, at one point, have been separated geographically by some cataclysm, the results of that separation would manifest themselves only gradually in the ensuing generations as they adapted themselves to their different environments.

The concept of species, then, seems more real to us than it otherwise would because what we see represents only a temporal cross-section of the Tree of Life. What we see in our present is only branch-ends, appearing separate from one another because their connections have disappeared from view with the extinction of the intervening forms. Even so, we experience difficulty when we try to apply our inherited system of classification to these branch-ends. For we are puzzled to know what respective distances between them represent, respectively, the graduated stages which we call subspecies, species, genera, families, etc., stages which we suppose to exist in nature.

The difficulty of fitting our system of classification to the phenomena of nature is enhanced by the fact that, in some cases, the intermediate forms have not disappeared. If, for example, we look at *Gray's New Manual*

of Botany (7th edition) we find that among the species
of the genus *Aster* it lists *macrophyllus, Herveyi,* and
spectabilis. Our inherited habit of thought is such that
we suppose these three species to be real, as if God had
made each as a separate creation. When we try to
identify specimens of them growing in the fields, however, we run into trouble. Any individual plant, dis-
sected and its parts examined under a microscope, may
prove to be intermediate, in its diagnostic character-
istics, between *macrophyllus* and *Herveyi* or between
Herveyi and *spectabilis.* Moreover, there is such a range
of variation within what is called the one species *macrophyllus* that some botanists have been tempted to divide
it into several species (viz., *pinquifolius, excelsior, velu-
tinus, sejunctus, apricensis, ianthinus, violaris, multi-
formis,* and *nobilis*).

Here in the Alps, where I am setting down these
observations, we continually run into the same problem. Finding a large blue gentian growing on the turf
below the melting snow, we tend to assume that it has
to be either the Stemless Gentian (*Gentiana Clusii*) or
the Carved Gentian (*G. Kochiana*). The fact that it
appears intermediate between the two makes no difference. We shall have to say which of the two it is when
we write up our notes; and so we argue whether it is
closer to *Clusii* (and therefore must in fact be *Clusii*)
or closer to *Kochiana* (and therefore must in fact be
Kochiana). "In fact" it is neither, since neither *Clusii*
nor *Kochiana* exists as a fact of nature, any more than
the distinct degrees on the scale of a thermometer exist
as facts of nature.

For reasons which it would be interesting to explore,
these present-day continuums in nature are less frequent in the animal kingdom, where the existing
branch-ends generally appear to be more distinctly
separated from one another; but they occur here too.
It may be that the Song Sparrow (*Melospiza melodia*),
in its variation from Maine to Arizona, represents a

continuum (which the taxonomic authorities have agreed to divide into twenty subspecies, although they might have divided it into more or fewer), and that the Maine and Arizona forms would be listed as two distinct species, respectively, if the intermediate forms had become extinct. When it comes to the Yellow Wagtail group in the Old World (*Motacilla flava*), the concept of species appears to break down completely, as it appears to do in the botanical genera *Aster* and *Solidago*.

The examples I have given here illustrate a philosophic principle. It is that we inhabit two worlds at once, a world of real phenomena, on the one hand, a world of nominal ideas on the other. The physical gentian growing out of the turf belongs to the world of real phenomena; *Clusii* or *Kochiana* belongs to the world of nominal ideas. The one exists in nature, the other only in our minds. *Motacilla flava*, likewise, is a nominal concept which cannot quite be made to fit the variegated reality to which we try to apply it.

To state the matter in its simplest terms, we may say that there are things and there are the names we attribute to things. The first are real in a sense in which the latter are not. When we argue about the identification of the gentian, then, we are not arguing about what it really is but, rather, about what to call it for the purpose of communicating or recording our observation. What we call it should tell us as much as possible about the reality, but it is not itself a reality.

Taxonomy undertakes to devise a nominal world that will fit the world of physical realities as closely as may be. This undertaking can never be more than partially successful, however, because of an inherent difference between the two worlds. The nominal world is by its nature a categorical world, while the real world is essentially uncategorical. *Motacilla flava* is a categorical term applied to uncategorical realities. In the nominal world the temperature goes up by categorical steps, by degrees Fahrenheit, while in the real world its variation is continuous. In the nominal world the branches of the Tree of Life diverge by categorical steps—by subspecies, species, genera, etc.—while in the real world they diverge continuously.

This is not to suggest that the world of nominal categories is necessarily a fraud. It is a fraud only when it presents itself to us as identical with the world of nature. Because of centuries-old habit, however, we are prone to confuse the two (to believe that God or nature created the Stemless Gentian and the Carved Gentian, each according to its kind). When we do this we tend to lose our grasp of reality and to end, perhaps, in a preoccupation with problems that are essentially irrelevant to it.

We understand nature more truly, then, when we bear in mind that its real existence is independent of the rough nominal description we make of it. Taxonomic systems are a necessity of human thought and understanding, but they can never be quite true to nature and should never, therefore, be taken literally.

It was Justice Oliver Wendell Holmes who admonished us to think things rather than words. While we cannot think without words in fact, we can at least understand their limitations in the act of using them.

Chemically, the face of our planet, the biosphere, is being sharply changed by man, consciously, and even more so, unconsciously. The aerial envelope of the land as well as all its natural waters are changed both physically and chemically by man. In the twentieth century, as a result of the growth of human civilization, the seas and the parts of the oceans closest to shore become changed more and more markedly. Man now must take more and more measures to preserve for future generations the wealth of the seas which so far have belonged to nobody. Besides this, new species and races of animals and plants are being created by man.

—from the translation of a paper by Academician V. I. Vernadsky, written in 1943, *American Scientist*, Vol. 33, No. 1, p. 1.

THE REFUGEE SPECIES

THE thesis of this article is that, in the rapidly developing circumstances of our age, the distinction between wild animals and those domestic to man is losing its sharpness if not disappearing altogether. This has its implications for the attitude that we human beings should properly take toward the other species, formerly wild and independent, which inhabit our planet alongside us.

What are the rapidly developing circumstances to which I refer?

For millions of years the earth was wild in the sense that it was the original, raw, natural earth, not fundamentally altered by any of the diverse species that occurred here and there on its surface. The species adjusted themselves to the local environments as they found them. This was true of the earliest men, too, when they began to emerge in the evolutionary process, perhaps a million years ago. Not until some seven thousand years ago, when our ancestors had learned the rudiments of agriculture, did they begin to reshape and reconstruct the environment. Then they cleared patches of wild forest and, by exhausting the soil, made occasional deserts.

Until the most recent times, however, our numbers were too small and weak to make any widespread difference in the earth's surface. Five hundred years ago the entire population of North America north of the Rio Grande (estimated at one and a half million) may have been less than the present population of greater Washington—which is to say that man had not yet effectively occupied a continental area representing more than one fifth of the earth's land-surface. Most of South America, most of Africa, and most of northern Asia were sparsely or only locally inhabited. Even the great population centers of modern times— China, India, the Mediterranean area, Europe—had only a small fraction of the population they support today.

Suddenly, in our own day, the human population has expanded and become dense, forming one continuous community all around the earth. As if at one stroke, our planet has virtually been wrapped in a layer of humanity. At the same time, this human population has embarked on an industrial revolution by which it has already, in an instant of history, gained command of the physical power to alter the entire face of the earth, raising the levels of the oceans if it should wish, splitting apart mountains, sterilizing continents. (The destructive uses of this power come the easiest. We can make a desert easier than unmake one.)

If one were to plot on a graph the growth of the human population over the centuries, and the growth of the physical power at its command, the resulting curves, almost horizontal to begin with, would bend upward more and more steeply, until in our own time they suddenly approached the vertical. (An estimated world population of 470 million in 1650 had increased to 2,406 million by 1950, and is hundreds of millions higher today.) This geometric acceleration of development has at last produced, in the twentieth century, what is surely the greatest crisis in the history of mankind, and one of the great crises in the history of all life on earth. It is our generation that lives in the midst of this crisis.

Philosophers since Hegel, at the beginning of the nineteenth century, observing how rapidly mankind has been mastering nature, have cast man in the role of the Creator, maintaining that the world is the product of his invention. Noting that man is on the verge of being able to create life synthetically, and that he is already able to create new species by conscious purpose, scientists like Sir Julian Huxley and the late Teilhard de Chardin have suggested that he is now becoming the master, not only of his own evolution, but of the evolution of life in general. He is able to decree life or death all over the earth.

While it is absurd, if not also monstrous, to attribute all creation to actual men, it is undeniable that the physical earth today—as one views it from an airplane —is in substantial part man-made. The continents have been given over to real-estate development. Where forests still stand they are likely to be, not the aboriginal forests, but woodlots kept and tended by the local population or by the state. Waterways have been artificially stabilized by dike and dam; swamps have been removed and lakes built; fields have been cleared, planted, and managed; even the atmosphere has been subjected to local pollution and is now being made more radioactive on a global scale. It is evident that all species are, increasingly, the inhabitants of a new man-made world, a world artificially remodeled by our kind for its own convenience. Everywhere, the land is enclosed and reserved for man. Only the sea remains wild, and even here the human impact is increasingly manifested: the great whales have, in some cases, been reduced to a remnant, pollution has altered local environments, and the signs of human activity are spreading in the deep.

From its beginning to our own day man's accelerating reconstruction of the earth's surface has not been a planned or conscious process. Here or there, our ancestors cut down the trees simply because they were in their way; they drained swamps, diked streams, and persecuted various species for immediate practical purposes only, unmindful of larger and longer consequences. By the late nineteenth century, however, it was no longer possible to disregard these consequences. In North America, where change had come most suddenly, and had therefore been most spectacular and destructive, the unthinking and unintended annihilation of species like the Passenger Pigeon, widespread erosion, the creation of "dust-bowl" deserts, the pollution of waterways, etc., were causes for alarm that compelled us to take account of the broader implications of what we were doing. When we did take account of them, we had to face the necessity of planning and control.

Our generation lives in the midst of the great crisis, and one of the turning-points that the crisis must represent is the shift from unplanned and uncontrolled to planned, organized, and controlled transformation of the earth. For better or worse, mankind is now assuming conscious direction of the earth's development and the evolution of life.

I admit to misgivings about this when I consider the limits of our collective wisdom, but it is unavoidable.

In this article I am concerned only with the status, in the man-made world of the future, of what we have been used to calling the creatures of the wild. If these creatures disappeared altogether the richness of our own human life would be diminished. Where they remain, however, they must be regarded as refugees from a vanished or vanishing world. Conscious provision must be made for their adjustment to the novel man-made environment which is so rapidly replacing the environment that belonged to them, that had been their home. Although it was never the case before, from now on they will have to live in a relation of dependence on man, we men will have to assume a responsibility for them not altogether unlike that we assume for our domestic animals. Under these circumstances, it is not too early for us to redefine their proper relationship to us and to the world that we have made ours.

At present, in this moment of transition, the situation is anomalous. I shall illustrate this by specific examples drawn from the locality in which I happen to live, but which could be duplicated all around the earth.

Let me first take that majestic bird, the Mute Swan. Its present status all over Europe and the British Isles may be representative of the status that we shall have to accord to other species in the future. It lives at large on all the lakes and waterways, building its nests and raising its young in freedom along the shores. Its members, however, enjoy a special status of quasi-domesticity. In the British Isles they have been the property of the crown for centuries, and as such they may not be molested. On the Lake of Geneva, in the Canton of Geneva where I live, they are under the protection and control of the state. They wear identifying bands on their legs, attached while they are still nestlings; a special functionary of the state keeps track of their numbers and guards their nesting sites; food is provided for them in the City of Geneva. These swans are largely dependent on human bounty, the people who live along the shores of the lake having acquired the habit of feeding them. A relation of confidence therefore exists between the human beings and the swans, the latter living in the ports and harbors of the former, showing no fear of them, taking bread from their hands, accepting their ministrations. All over Europe the swans have been legally adopted by the human communities and have become essentially domestic, although without losing their freedom.

Another example of what is, in a sense, domestication, is that of the House Sparrow, which exists hardly anywhere, today, outside the closest association with human communities; which has, in fact, spread its numbers around the globe with the spread of human civilization—in man's baggage, so to speak.

A less extreme example would be that of the small Black-headed Gull which, partly in consequence of human care, has now become the commonest gull in Europe. Its individuals also live largely in human communities and are city birds. They scavenge in the harbors of London and Geneva alike. They are fed from the embankments of the Thames, the Seine, and the Rhône. In Geneva they are even found in the city streets with pigeons, and patrol the upper stories of the apartment-houses, where they are fed from windows and balconies. They too have been brought into the man-made world, have been given a status in it, are protected, and have gained enough confidence to take food from the hand. The line between wild and domestic, with respect to them, has at least been blurred.

Now let me cite an example of the anomaly that represents the transition in which we live. Thousands of wild ducks winter on the Lake of Geneva, many of them about the docks and piers of Geneva and other towns. Flocks of one species, the Pochard, commonly sleep during the day, head under wing, in the heart of Geneva, beside a bridge over which the heavy traffic rumbles continuously. The pedestrians on the bridge may watch them from only a few feet away. Within the official city-limits, the Pochards and other wild ducks are protected and fed like the swans. But just outside those limits, which the city has long since overspread, they are freely shot by hunters who range the embankments with shotguns or go out after them in boats. About four miles from the city a minuscule marsh has been set aside as a sanctuary for waterfowl; but some hundred yards from it a duck-blind has now been anchored in the lake; the ducks and other waterfowl going in and out of the sanctuary have to pass through the fire of the hunters.[1]

The anomaly is evident. On the one hand, these waterfowl, for whom there is no longer a wild environment left, are being welcomed into the new man-made environment that has succeeded to it. A place is being made for them in it, and they are being taught to confide themselves to it, as they do readily. On the other hand, the habit of exploiting them as aliens from the alien world of the wilderness persists. At one point along the shore they are cherished and accepted in domesticity; a few feet farther on they are shot by hunters who can approach them the more easily because of the confidence they have been taught. (The hunters are serving an impulse that may be said to be, in one sense, disinterested, for many of them have no means of retrieving the birds they wound or kill.)

In the case of some species the decimation of their numbers is itself a cause for distress. For example, not one of the few Eiders that come from the north each fall to winter on the Lake of Geneva survives to go north again in the spring. They are so approachable, and therefore so easily shot, that none are left by the middle of January.

Another example. Geese have largely disappeared

[1] Since this article was written these practices have been radically restricted by law in Geneva.

over the continent of Europe, but early in January of last year a flock of Bean Geese, extraordinarily large for our times (although small by contrast with what used to be seen) showed up in the vicinity of Geneva. Immediately the hunters went after it. On January 15 the flock numbered over eighty-five. Two weeks later it was down to thirty. By February 25 it was down to twelve. These geese would have had the same experience virtually anywhere they had tried to winter in Europe. Their problem is that their natural world is gone and, through a failure of human awareness and responsibility, no room has yet been made for them in the man-made world that has replaced it.

I am not concerned here exclusively or even primarily with the danger of extinction that faces species for which the necessary accommodation has not been made. I am concerned that we men complete the transition to the man-made world by consciously establishing a new relationship with the refugee remnants from the vanished wilderness. The thousands of common ducks that winter on the Lake of Geneva are in no present danger of extinction. But there is something in the business of shooting them—where they have come to depend on our hospitality, where we have been welcoming and domesticating them—that should weigh on our consciences.

At the beginning of November, before the hunting has got under way, I go out in my boat on the lake and observe the waterfowl regaling themselves on the surface, essentially undisturbed by my own peaceful passage among them. Two weeks later when I put out on the lake they take off in alarm for half a mile around, filling the sky in their hundreds and thousands, circling back and forth over the hiding places where the hunters, waiting to bring them down, profit by the disturbance I have so unwillingly created. The guns go off, the ducks fall, and I feel myself part of a betrayal that is discreditable to us all.

It is tempting to regard the hunters as evil men, which they are not. They are simply men like the rest of us who have not yet realized in their own minds the revolutionary transformation that has taken place in the world. They are still responding to the obsolete impulse of ancestors who lived in the wild world and pitted themselves against it. They are still responding to this impulse at a time when what represents the wild world has been reduced to a disorganized remnant of refugees, like human refugees from a city struck by disaster.

The hunters and what they represent are disappearing, more rapidly in some countries, less so in others. (Switzerland is well ahead of France, which in turn is ahead of Italy.) They are a dwindling minority alongside the increasing numbers of those who look upon their victims as wards of the human community and consequently feel the essential shamefulness of their sport. Year by year the adjustment is made. This year, for example, a new federal law in Switzerland has closed the hunting-season on waterfowl at the end of January, instead of at the end of February as heretofore. More and more, the ordinary men in the street, listening to the guns and seeing the birds fall, express their concern that the creatures who have taken refuge in the human communities should be shot at all. In time it will be stopped altogether, because under the new circumstances that we men have hardly yet grasped the offense that it represents becomes constantly more obvious.

The change takes place first in the human mind, responding belatedly to the changed environment. Something more is demanded of us today, however, than the unconscious process of adaptation from generation to generation that was sufficient for a world in slower transformation. The present challenge is such that the response, to be adequate, must be deliberately organized and planned.

The provision that should be made is as various as the species to be provided for. Many species—e.g., the House Sparrow, the Chimney Swift, the Gray Squirrel, the Rhesus Monkey—have already adapted themselves to our world, with or without our help, and are at home in it. At the other extreme are species which can hardly be accommodated at all in the environment that we men make for ourselves. One thinks of the big cats and other large mammals, many of them native to Africa. If they are to survive, preserves of their natural environment will have to be set aside and artificially maintained, like zoological gardens on a vast scale for the exhibition of the wilderness that once was.

Most of the species that interest us, however, fall between these extremes, and to them the example of the swans may be relevant. Where they are not persecuted, these species will generally adapt themselves readily to a human environment—as in the case of the ducks in the harbor of Geneva. Peregrine Falcons, which we think of as epitomizing the splendor of the wild, take naturally to the tall buildings of our big cities (so like their native cliffs) and, with easily made provision for nesting-sites, would surely become established among them. There is no reason why the American Eagle, which used to be seen in winter on cakes of ice off Manhattan, which may still be seen about Washington, should not become as much a city bird as the Herring Gull, except that it is disappearing at such a cataclysmic rate (apparently because of sterility caused by the new insecticides spread by man) that it may be too late to save it.[2] I myself have seen that denizen of the wilderness, the Short-eared Owl, hunting locusts on the lawns of a crowded park

[2] Since this was written the Peregrine Falcon has disappeared completely from eastern North America and is on its way to extinction all over the world, the victim of environmental pollution by man. The same thing is happening to the American Eagle, the Osprey, and other species.

in the center of Buenos Aires, despite the persecution of little boys who threw stones at it. This past January, when exceptionally heavy snow covered the usual hunting-grounds of the European Buzzards, closely related to our Red-tailed Hawk, they invaded the City of Geneva, making themselves at home in its parks and gardens.

In England, which is further advanced than any other country in the protection of wildlife, species that are notable for their shyness elsewhere have become almost as domestic as the swans. Among us, no bird is shyer and wilder than the Florida Gallinule, and it tends to be the same on the continent; but in England, where it is known as the Moorhen, it walks about one's feet in parks and gardens. Last October I saw a migrating Cormorant land on the little pond in London's St. James's Park, amid swarms of people. The European Robin, a shy woodland bird on the continent, shows what appears outwardly as an almost affectionate affinity for human beings in England, to the point of following them about and keeping close to them. What this demonstrates is that the cessation of persecution alone is enough to bring many of the species of the disappearing wilderness into a relationship with us similar to that of the swans.

The present status of the Mute Swan in Europe represents what may prove to be, with variations, the most satisfactory arrangement for a large number of birds and mammals that are losing their native habitats. The species that fall into this category must be accepted as semi-domesticated wards that justify their protection and such maintenance as they require by the interest, the variety, and the beauty that they contribute to an environment which would be desolate without them.

Perhaps we ought to draw up, on a worldwide scale and under the auspices of international organization, a charter for the refugee species, establishing categories among them and suggesting the type of provision to be made for each category. Our respective governments might then be encouraged and helped to give effect to the charter in their several jurisdictions all around the globe.

THE PARISH OF AMERICA

In his monograph on the birds of southern South America, Alexander Wetmore reported arriving in Buenos Aires in the year 1920 after a twenty-four-day journey from New York. In September 1947 I arrived in Buenos Aires after a two-day journey from Washington, D.C. This shrinkage of the earth in the course of a generation should enlarge our understanding of the birds that inhabit it, for we can now accompany them with a new ease across the old horizons. Gilbert White, had he lived in 1947, might have taken the western hemisphere for his parish, instead of Selborne. He would not then have wondered what happened to swallows in winter.

My visit to South America prompted the reflection that our minds have not yet taken advantage of this speed and ease with which we now reduce distance. We look at birds with an eye that is still parochial on the old scale, losing sight of them when they cross the horizons of our Selborne.

Of course, we did not have to wait for the airplane to learn where our birds wintered. We knew that—rather, we knew of it. The airplane now makes it easy to see their winter background and how they live in it; it takes you along with them to what had been a never-never land. When you have seen a Solitary Sandpiper in the same landscape with Rheas it looks different the next time you see it along a New England brook; it will never again be just a North American bird. This represents an improvement in your understanding, because it never was. When you have seen robins from Mexico to Argentina—brown robins, gray robins, black robins, big robins, little robins—you come to look at our own red-breasted Robin as the local representative of a certain group having a certain background, which is what it always has been.

Habitat, natural environment, is an essential characteristic of species. The fact that a bird inhabits
swamps defines it as much as does the color of its
eyes or the length of its rectrices. That is the reason
for habitat-groups in our museums; that is why the
birds of these habitat-groups are more accurately represented—more "to the life"—than the live birds in a
zoo. A gull in a cage is not a gull; the ecologist does
not recognize it.

The total environment of many familiar American
birds has now become casually accessible for the first
time. I do not mean that all of us can extend our bird-
walks to South America, but enough of us can do so
to give the others that experience vicariously. As it is,
however, our popular bird-books, if they do mention
that a certain species winters in southern Brazil, report
on it only in its northern home. They report on half
the whole bird. In all that concerns our appreciation
of it, it vanishes when it crosses our border.

Edwin Way Teale undertook to follow the advancing
spring season of 1947 from the southern tip of Florida
to New England (and he has promised to let us have
a book on it).[1] When I saw him in Washington, however, I was able to supplement his observations because
I had followed that same season from Panamá to
Mexico and Cuba, turning it over to him, as I maintained, only after it had crossed the Tropic of Cancer.
I had seen Redstarts and Kentucky Warblers on their
way through Costa Rica that he may have seen later
against a different background. He is an indulgent
man with a sense of humor, so there was no danger
of his resenting my assumed arrogance when I insisted
that, for all his determination to witness the season's
progress from its very beginning, he had come late.

William Vogt and I have, for some time now, joined
our forces in a campaign to have Roger Tory Peterson
enlarge his parish by crossing the Rio Grande. This

[1] Later published as *North with the Spring*, New York, 1951.

article will have served a practical purpose if it brings in recruits or in any way stimulates more of our nature-writers and artists to take bird-walks in lands to the south. With the publication of the latest in Peterson's series of "Field Guides to the Birds," further development along these lines in North America would be painting the lily. Except for two or three local beginnings, however, the Field Guides and Handbooks for Middle and South America remain to be done. Their doing would be useful, not only for those who live or visit in those countries, but for our fuller knowledge of the birds in our own country. This, I hold, should be the great new development.

It has slowly dawned on me, in the course of successive visits to Latin America, that the bird-life of the hemisphere is more uniform than I had thought. For example, when I first saw birds below the Rio Grande one that immediately attracted my attention was a large, noisy flycatcher with yellow underparts and a black-and-white head. At first I thought of this species, my experience being so limited, as one that occurs from sea-level to about five thousand feet on the eastern slope of Guatemala. I was, in this respect, like the man who named the Kentucky Warbler. Today I know this same "local" bird as one of the most conspicuously common in the hemisphere, called the Derby or Kiskadee Flycatcher in our southwest and the *bien-te-veo* in Argentina. It has served me as a reliable alarm clock in Mexico, in Buenos Aires, and at points in between.

Upon that first arrival in Latin America, years ago, I saw another fine flycatcher within half an hour of my landing that sent me combing in vain through Griscom's *Distribution of Bird-life in Guatemala*—in vain, because that fine monograph offers no clues for identification. I should have done better to look through a guide to the birds of our own West, for my bird was

Tyrannus melancholicus, variously known as Couch's Kingbird, Lichtenstein's Kingbird, and the Olive-backed Kingbird (there should be a law against more than one common name per language per species)—or through W. H. Hudson's *Birds of La Plata,* where it appears as the Bellicose Tyrant. It occurs in Texas and Arizona; but the last time I saw it was in Paraguay.

Having had no opportunity to see the Vermilion Flycatcher in our own southwest, I think of it as the *Churrinche* of Argentina. Others know it only as a southwestern bird. It is, of course, a bird of the western hemisphere between the latitudes of snow.

An example of our unthinking parochialism is that we often refer to such species as the Everglade Kite, the Swallow-tailed Kite, and the Roseate Spoonbill as verging on extinction. I found the Everglade Kite common on the pampas; the Swallow-tailed Kite occurs in numbers throughout a large part of the hemisphere; and the spoonbill may well be one of the commoner large birds of the hemisphere. Many birds, like these, are not so much North American species as South American species that spill over into our land. We easily forget that North America is only one corner of a bird's-eye view.

I judge that the sharpest line of demarcation in the western hemisphere, speaking in terms of ranges rather than habitats, is the Rio Grande, and that is not so very sharp. Certain groups that are exceptionally prominent in the avifauna south of it—notably the woodhewers and ovenbirds (*Dendrocolaptidae* and *Furnariidae*)—do not cross it, but almost all others at least spill over from both sides. Migration, however, binds the parts of the hemisphere together, making it one parish if nothing else does. The best place to see our Golden Plover, since abundance counts, is on the Argentine pampas during the months in which they are not breeding. Our Yellow-legs, Greater and Lesser, winter from the southern United States to Patagonia.

(To anyone who sees them in Argentina they are summering, or at least wintering in summer. The Argentines might think of them as wintering in the United States. How many of our birds live in an eternal summer!)

It is true, of course, that in large parts of the American tropics a stranger from the north might on first arrival be hardly more at home among the birds than in New Guinea. The tropical rain-forest, as a habitat, has resident birds that are peculiar to it and could not be found in countries like ours where that habitat does not exist. In addition to the large groups that come within this category, there are individual species with narrowly restricted ranges. Even if they are not all represented in the United States, however, the traveler in the American tropics learns by increasing experience how few are local and how wide are the ranges of many. The Blue Tanager is as common in Paraguay as in Guatemala. A sparrow of the genus *Zonotrichia* is one of the commonest songbirds in practically every city of Latin America from Guatemala (I have not seen it in Mexico City) to the southern tip of South America, including La Paz, 12,500 feet high in the Andes. True, it is not all one species, but the several species are so closely related in song and appearance that they may be regarded as varieties of one type. Like the Kiskadee Flycatcher, it makes the traveler from Guatemala feel at home in Buenos Aires.

Other birds that our familiarity with Hudson has led us to associate exclusively with the pampas are, in fact, found in the grasslands of almost any part of South America. I did not have to go as far as the pampas to see the Spur-winged Lapwing. It was no less common in central Paraguay, when I went there from Argentina. It was waiting for me at the airport of Campo Grande in the Matto Grosso of Brazil. There it was again at the airport of Puerto Suarez, on the eastern border of Bolivia. Three days later I saw it yet again on the *altiplano* of Bolivia, at 13,500 feet (where I also came upon a Black-crowned Night Heron). When I looked it up, on my return to Washington, I found that I could have seen it as well on the grasslands of Venezuela, four hours from the United States. The big gray-and-white Eagle Hawks that occur throughout southern Argentina were common on the coast of Peru.

The coast of Peru, in turn, is extraordinarily like the coast of California: cool, arid, foggy, fertile where watered, Spanish colonial background, barren mountains coming down to the sea, precipitous islets just offshore. Both coasts swarm with seabirds. Both have a native condor. The Least Tern, when it goes from summer in California to summer in Peru, might simply be passing through the looking glass.

Nothing I have reported here is not perfectly well known to all our ornithologists who have studied in South and Central America; but they are scientists, and what they give us are monographs that presuppose a technical knowledge of the birds in that area. Popular writers have confined themselves to our old parish, now out of date. The world has become as small for us as it always has been for the birds, but our popular practice has not caught up with them. The time has come at last to follow these fellow parishioners of ours to the ends of their parish, our new parish, disregarding political and geographic boundaries that were never known to their ancient "winged nation."

FOR most readers of bird literature, the pampas of Argentina have a sort of legendary existence. They are known as the subject of W. H. Hudson's finest descriptive writing—the finest description, I would say, that has been lavished on any region and its birds. Hudson left South America, never to return, in 1874, and when he wrote about the pampas and the birds of the pampas in later years he wrote about what he thought had gone forever from the earth. The scene lived intact, he believed, only in his memory. Few phrases have been more nostalgic than the last sentence of his chapter about bird migration on the pampas: "The beautiful has vanished and returns not."[1]

I think the distress Hudson felt in faraway England at reports of what was happening to wildlife on the pampas led him into some exaggeration. This possibility had not occurred to me, however, when I took 'plane for Buenos Aires in September 1947. I did not expect so much to revisit the past as the scene of the past —a prospect exciting enough in itself. Although I assumed that the once abundant population of large birds like rheas, Crested Screamers, Spur-winged Lapwings, and storks would be rare at best and to be found, if at all, in places almost beyond reach of civilization, I hoped that I might at least hear the songs of mockingbirds and thrushes described by Hudson. With luck I might find the Argentine Ovenbird and the clay oven it constructs for a nest, or the big Guira Cuckoo. There would certainly be pieces of the past, shards and flints, left at this scene of the past.

My expectations were also held in check by the knowledge that I would have little opportunity to

---

[1] The quotations of Hudson are from *A Hind in Richmond Park*, Chap. XI.

search for birds—that I could not, at any rate, reach the remote places where I might hope to find remnants of the larger wildlife described by Hudson. It is only two days from Washington, D.C., to Buenos Aires now, but the tempo of life matches the speed of travel, so that one turns around and comes back as quickly. The time saved by air-travel has not brought leisure, it has rather done away with it. Circumstances, however, presented me with five days of freedom between the conclusion of official business in Buenos Aires and my departure for another country. It was the beginning of spring, although fall at home, and I had, in fact, arrived on the first full day of the new season, of nature's new year, in time to see black locusts and wistaria in bloom and the leaves just emerging from their buds on the plane trees of Buenos Aires. I carried letters of introduction to Dr. Jorge Casares, a leading ornithologist of Argentina and a man of great hospitality, and to Dr. Fernando Pozzo, the translator of Hudson into Spanish, who is the active leader of a small group of Argentines that undertook, some years ago, to promote an appreciation of Hudson in his native land, where he remained without honor long after his fame had been established in England and North America.

My first view of the pampas was on a Sunday afternoon's visit with Dr. and Mrs. Pozzo to the site of Hudson's natal home, "Los Veinte-cinco Ombúes" (The Twenty-five Ombú Trees), on the Arroyo Conchitas. The first chapter of *Far Away and Long Ago* has a description of the site, in a place where the flat pampas swell up to a low eminence that gives a view over miles of grassland in every direction. The grass is uniformly cropped by grazing cattle, but the cardoon thistles remembered by Hudson form thick clumps all over the ground, so crowded that they interfere with walking. They are of the two common types that Hudson mentions: the Cardoon of Castille, which has gray leaves, and the Giant Thistle, its green leaves splotched or vermiculated with white (the legend is that Mary, fleeing from Egypt with the Infant Christ, spilled some of her milk on them; hence the scientific name: *Silybum marianum*).

The brook, which is still called Conchitas, appears at the foot of the slope as a line of thick green rushes crossing the plain. Such streams are typical of the pampas, distinguishing them from other extensive flatlands grazed by cattle like those in the panhandle of Texas. They are marshy streams, often quite deep and imperceptibly below the level of the surrounding land.

It must be remembered that basic changes in the pampas occurred before Hudson's day. "Few countries," Darwin wrote, "have undergone more remarkable changes, since the year 1535, when the first colonist of La Plata landed with seventy-two horses. The countless herds of horses, cattle, and sheep, not only have altered the whole aspect of the vegetation, but they have almost banished the guanaco, deer, and ostrich."[2] I judge that the chief superficial difference brought about in the last century is in the number of exotic trees distributed in groves of varying size across the pampas. Such groves had been planted before Hudson's day but must be commoner now. They resemble archipelagos in the smooth sea of the pampas. Although it was still the cool season, the mirage was a conspicuous feature of the midday landscape: a shining area in the distance that might have been water and that reflected the silhouettes of Lombardy poplars and other trees "hull-down" along the horizon. Made dim by distance, the trees and their inverted reflections appeared to be continuously changing shape in the shimmer of the mirage.

Two ancient Ombú trees on the site may be the last of the "Twenty-five Ombús," but perhaps the species is

---

[2] *The Voyage of the Beagle*, Chap. VI.

not so long-lived. The Ombú, I am told, has no cambium layer and is not properly a tree, although large and stout enough in appearance. Its roots grow together to form a platform well above the ground, from which several trunks rise, making each tree seem like a small grove—an excellent place for children to play, as Hudson noted. The leaves were just beginning to appear when I saw them.

The only building on the site today is a low whitewashed house, built from a kind of adobe brick that was used anciently, so that there is reason to believe it was standing in Hudson's time. Dr. Pozzo believes it was the Hudson residence, but I agree with those who think it was an incidental building, perhaps for peons. The family that inhabits it today might be the reincarnation of some gaucho family described by Hudson, the man with baggy trousers and long mustachios, the women sipping maté from a gourd.

I have not mentioned the birds that are so prominent a feature in the scenery of the pampas until now because I got to know them more fully later, when Dr. and Mrs. Casares took me to visit large *estancias* in Buenos Aires Province and to stay overnight at the hospitable Pearson *estancia*, "El Destino," near the mouth of the Plate estuary. Here, outside the urban influence of Buenos Aires, the incomparable wealth of bird life reported by Hudson, or what is left of it, is on display.

"South America," Hudson wrote, "can well be called the great bird continent, and I do not believe that any other large area on it so abounded with bird life as this very one where I was born and reared and saw, and heard, so much of birds from my childhood that they became to me the most interesting things in the world."

The pampas still abound with birds. I mean by this that one looks out over them and sees birds everywhere, big birds standing on the cropped pasture, birds running or walking, birds soaring or flapping, circling above, flying past in flocks, flitting over the grass, rising, dropping. Some are familiar. The flocks of Shiny Cowbirds resemble our common North American Cowbird on the wing, though their uniformly purple-black plumage shines like metal. I think our Cowbird is not so common anywhere. The Yellow-shouldered Marsh Birds in the rushes along the brooks are the same as our Redwings, except for the bright yellow that replaces the red and brown. The abundant doves of four or five species range in size from the little Torcacita to others larger than our domestic pigeon, and one of the commonest belongs to the genus of our Mourning Dove. The commoner of two local harriers (*Circus cinereus*) resembles our Marsh Hawk. My best view of our own Short-eared Owl was of one hunting locusts in a city park of Buenos Aires, on a Saturday afternoon when it was crowded, but they are well known throughout the open country. American and Snowy Egrets are occasional on the pampas, although not so common as I find them in other parts of South America (I am speaking, of course, only for what I saw in Argentina at the time I saw it). Students of Florida birds would recognize Burrowing Owls and Everglade Kites; the kitchen-middens of the kites are found everywhere, heaps of empty snail-shells at the foot of fence-posts. The Florida students would also recognize the Limpkin and probably take it for the same species as ours. It is, in fact, a closely allied species.

None of these birds are among the most conspicuous or striking. On the open pampas I think first honors go to the Spur-winged Lapwing, a boldly marked, long-legged plover the size of a teal, with big rounded wings of contrasting gray, black, and white, that makes a great commotion and noisy display of energy to tell the trespasser that he is trespassing

(*terú, terú* in lapwing language). The Chimangos (a small caracara) come next, I think, although they are even more abundant in open groves of trees. They often appear mad with excess energy, small flocks diving upon one another, plunging to earth and swooping upward again, screaming incessantly. The large caracaras or Caranchos are not so numerous, longer in the neck, and more dignified. Where there is a dead cow you ordinarily see a pair of them feasting. They, with the Chimangos, replace our vultures, of which I saw none.

If you let your gaze sweep over the pampas, the chances are good that you will see one or more Maguari Storks, like the European stork in appearance, standing or walking with sober dignity, or perhaps circling aloft with the same dignity and ease. The chances are equally good that you will see a pair of large dark birds simply standing, some distance apart from each other. These are the Crested Screamers, almost as large as swans and like nothing else outside of South America. Thomas Huxley thought them modern relatives of the Archeopteryx. These screamers, like all the big birds that stand on the open ground, generally allow you to come close enough for a detailed view before they take flight, and then flap off only a short distance to put down again and let you repeat your approach. They protest with loud cries of *chahá* as they take off, flapping their big wings heavily and making apparently slow progress for all their effort. It would be no trick to shoot them, and since Hudson reported that they were palatable I attribute their survival in such numbers to the abundance of excellent beef that makes Argentina a gourmet's paradise. I recall, however, seeing two freshly shot screamers hanging from the saddle-bow of a mounted soldier on the pampas.

One screamer was on a big nest that had been built up in a marshy stream above the level of the water, its mate standing on dry land nearby. We drove it from the nest to reveal its two eggs. Both birds flapped off some distance and then stood screaming *chahá* in mechanical fashion until we moved away, allowing them to return. Another pair were shepherding four young already the size of Canada Geese. We drove the parents off and caught one of the young, with little difficulty, to be photographed and to have the two big spurs on each wing examined by us. When we let it go it ran with a lumbering gait after its family, saying as plainly as possible in its whole manner, "Wait for me, wait for me!"

As you go out across the pampas you discover that in large parts they are thinly covered or blanketed by a continuous flock of Golden Plovers, which run in short stages across the flat ground. They had arrived a couple of weeks earlier on their migration from North America and still showed remnants of the breeding plumage. Other large plovers of a local species, the Slender-billed Plover, were sparsely mixed among them.

The Spotted Tinamou, a most delicate creature, hides or runs in the grass but flushes like a quail when you come close enough. It whirls off, its wings clattering in the air, to drop again into the grass beyond.

If the birds are generally common on the dry pampas, they are crowded in the stream beds among the rushes. The nesting screamers described above did not lack company. Here the lapwings are gathered in flocks associated with flocks of ducks (local species of pintail, teal, and widgeon) and sandpipers of various species, including our wintering Greater and Lesser Yellowlegs. Half a dozen or more Patagonian Black-headed Gulls will also be of the company, to say nothing of blackbirds (including the red-breasted Military Starling, so-called), Fork-tailed Flycatchers, and other passerine birds. Those who have seen the habitat-group of typical bird-life at a marshy place on the pampas, in New York's American Museum of Natural History, would find the actuality hardly less crowded.

I am told that only three kinds of tree, beside the Ombú, are native to the pampas. One of these is the Tala, a gnarled and thorny gray tree (its leaves had not yet started in early October) that grows in dense groves. The longtailed Monk Parakeets build huge apartment-house nests of briars in these trees, irregularly shaped and with separate entrances to the several apartments. Members of the community are seen climbing about the structure, and heard too. They are destructive to crops and so accounted a nuisance by the natives, who cannot appreciate their beauty with the unprejudiced eye of the visitor.

My purpose is little more than to suggest the wealth of birds that still remains from a time that had become legendary to Hudson, and so to his readers. The pampas, however, are only one part of the grassy plain that stretches from the southern tip of South America across Argentina, Uruguay, and western Paraguay into the Bolivian Chaco and the Matto Grosso of Brazil, where I saw the last of it. The bird-life of these grasslands has a basic uniformity. Species that are dominant in one locality may be relatively scarce a thousand miles farther north, or may be replaced by some closely allied species, but there is no such change as is immediately apparent when, as I later did, one crosses the Andes to the coast of Peru.

A hundred miles south of Buenos Aires, at the

marshes of Chascomús, I understand that I could
have found the Black-necked Swans, flamingos, and
Roseate Spoonbills that Hudson knew closer to Buenos
Aires. I went north instead, to Asunción and the
Province of Misiónes in Paraguay, where on an *estancia* owned by the Paraguayan Government I found the
greatest abundance and variety of birds I had ever
seen—of large birds at least—exceeding the pampas
themselves in this respect. The screamer is known
here, as are the flamingo and Jabiru Stork, but these
species are relatively rare and I saw none in my brief
stay. The adobe ranch-house is on an elevation in the
midst of a fertile valley rimmed by purple mountains
and cumulus clouds. As one's eyes travel over this immensity, from foreground to faraway distance, the
grazing cattle in scattered herds are reduced in perspective to mere specks. Binoculars reveal that the
rolling plain for miles is crowded with birds, most conspicuous of which are the white Maguari Storks. Here,
on dry pasture, I found the Black-faced Ibis and heard
its clanging cry as I repeatedly drove a pair to take
flight and settle again—a heavy-bodied bird for an ibis,
with short legs; the lovely Whistling Heron, like most
of these birds always in pairs; the great Eagle Hawks
in varying shades of pearl-gray, sometimes with white
bellies, nearly the most beautiful of the large hawks
I think; and others too numerous to mention here; as
well as the lapwings, the Chimangos, and many more
birds that I had been seeing in Argentina. The Chimangos were hardly less abundant than on the pampas, but here they competed with the equally abundant
Caranchos, Yellow-headed Caracaras, Black Vultures,

and Turkey Vultures. (One of the Yellow-headed Ca-racaras alighted on the back of a grazing cow that paid no attention.) To this list of carrion birds I add the Yellow-headed Vulture, apparently identical with the Turkey Vulture except for the color of its head, of which I saw one perched on a fence-post.

The climax of my delight at this scene, however, came with the discovery that Rheas or American Os-triches were common here, in flocks of up to half a dozen. The first I saw were five in a row on the crest of a hill, silhouetted against the sky, then running along the skyline in single file. This custom they have of forming in single file when they travel is nothing short of entrancing. I indulged in a piece of pleasant research, at my first opportunity, to determine how they cope with the occasional fence that bars their way. On horseback I galloped after a flock of six, herding them like mustangs against the angle formed by the juncture of two fences. They ran up and down before one of them (a five-strand wire fence) in ap-parent great agitation, poking their heads between the wires and trying to force a way through. Each of them, after several tries, burst through and raced away, but one did not find its way through till I had ridden to within thirty feet. I am told that it is only under the stress of some such emergency that they get through at all, and that they sometimes break the wires by sheer force.

I have hardly mentioned, till now, any birds that are not peculiar to the open pampas, that are not also found elsewhere, which means all the passerine spe-cies I saw except the Cachila Pipit and Military Star-ling, and numerous birds of other orders. While many of these birds do occur on the open pampas, and most of them are certainly found in the Tala groves, they are found almost everywhere else in varying quantities. The national bird of Argentina, by general consent, is the Hornero or Ovenbird, belonging to a common passerine family of the New World, *Furnariidae*, that is, nevertheless, without a representative north of the Rio Grande. It is the first bird you are likely to hear when you reach Argentina, at least in spring, for the pairs are constantly indulging in a shrill and clamorous mutual display, with much wing-shaking, the principal vocal feature of which is a note rapidly repeated on one pitch to form a near trill that falls off at the end. It is not a musical performance.

The Ovenbird is the size of our Starling and walks about on the grass like a Starling, but with a hesitant, high-strutting gait that is all its own. The most remarkable thing about it is the clay oven it constructs for its nest. You see these everywhere, on almost every exposed space from the horizontal limb of a tree to the cornice of a building, but especially on telegraph-poles. The gigantic stick-nests of the Leñatero or Firewood Gatherer, a small bird of the same family, are equally conspicuous if not so frequent in the road-side trees.

The prime competitor of the Ovenbird in noise-making is the Kiskadee Flycatcher, with its constantly iterated *bien-te-ve* or *kiskadee*, which is as noisily conspicuous here as throughout its range into Texas and Arizona. If the Ovenbird is the national bird of Argentina, perhaps this Bien-te-veo, as it is called in Spanish, might be considered the Pan-American bird.

I can only mention the lovely Forktailed Flycatcher and that darling among birds, the Vermilion Flycatcher, in passing. Neither is uncommon. Two birds that surprised me, and that I came to delight in, must be dealt with at greater length. One is the size of our Bluebird and the shape of a Robin, yellow beneath with a white throat, brown above. It seems most at home on lawns, like our Robin, where it makes running dashes to capture insects in the grass without rising on the wing. It also associates with cattle, like our Cowbird. I thought it likely that this unknown bird, called

"Papamosca," was a thrush, but it turned out to be a flycatcher, the Short-winged Tyrant.

The other bird is also found running about on the grassy pasture, although I first saw it in reed-beds bordering the River Plate. The size of a large sparrow, but with a delicate shape and graceful, alert manner, it is jet black as seen on the ground except for its pale yellow bill and a broad eye-ring or rosette of the same color, which gives it the appearance of wearing spectacles. When it flies, however, which it does for short distances in a bouncing manner, it displays snow-white primaries to contrast with the blackness. Unlikely as it seems, this is also a flycatcher, the Pico de Plata or Silverbill, sometimes called "the collegian" on account of its black dress and spectacles.

While I am on the subject of unlikely flycatchers I must mention the bird that gave me the greatest trouble in identification. It was a mockingbird in its behavior, general shape, and markings, with the same white flashes in its wings that our Mockingbird has and the white-tipped tail of Argentina's Calandria Mockingbird. I could not, however, make it fit the descriptions of any of the three mockingbirds that are found in Argentina, and I did not suppose that I had discovered a new species. The dilemma was resolved only when I drew a picture of it and showed it to Dr. Casares, who identified my bird as the Pepoaza Tyrant. I have become an ever greater admirer of the flycatcher family, which confines itself to the New World and there shows such versatility that its members range from near-kingfishers through near-swallows to mock mockingbirds.

Among the commonest birds that one finds everywhere, the Calandria Mockingbird is one of the most notable. Hudson rated its song second to that of its rarer congener, the White-banded Mockingbird, which I did not find. I heard the calandria sing only once, although it was so common, and then I was surprised by the loud, ringing sweetness of its song and the phrasing, which seemed to me to resemble that of the Nightingale.

The commonest Argentine robin, the Red-bellied Thrush, had just arrived on its migration from farther north, but though I saw many I heard none utter a sound. They have the excellent manners of our Robin and are, in fact, counterparts of our Robin in all but coloring, the upper parts being gray, the throat and breast white, the belly red.

The Guira Cuckoo is one of the commonest birds in city and country alike. A large, boldly marked, long-tailed, crested bird with the shape and manners of an ani—or as if an ani had been crossed with a Road-runner—it moves about in noisy flocks, like Blue Jays, and runs on the ground in spite of its short feet. It is clumsy and ludicrous, however, especially in its land-ings on the ground, when it almost invariably tips for-ward onto its nose, its long tail swinging up over its back. It tries to save itself from these unhappy land-ings by running rapidly as soon as it touches, but its landing gear is inadequate.

The Argentine Cardinal is like ours in size and shape, as well as in the color of its crested head and throat. Its underparts are white, however, its back and wings pearl gray. It is a garden bird, to be found about the edges of shrubbery anywhere, but it comes out into the open more than our Cardinal and walks on the ground instead of hopping. The song resembles that of our Scarlet Tanager or Rose-breasted Grosbeak rather than the separated notes and phrases of our own Cardinal. Other common garden birds are the Black-headed Siskin, a goldfinch with a black head, and the Blue-and-yellow Tanager, which is perhaps the most colorful of common Argentine birds, superficially resembling the beautiful tropical tanagers of the genus *Tangara*.

Throughout almost every city and settled place that

I know in the American continents from Guatemala south, one of the commonest birds is a sparrow of the genus *Zonotrichia*, to which our White-throated Sparrow belongs. It is not the same race or even the same species throughout, but the resemblances exceed the differences, and it is interesting to note the variations in its song as one travels from country to country. In Argentina it is well known as the Chingolo, and here it has a crest that it raises when alert, which it almost always is. The song is thin and simple, but musical, and one hears it everywhere all the time. It is as constant a singer as our own Song Sparrow is in season, but commoner and more widespread.

Apparently only one common woodpecker occurs in Buenos Aires Province, the Pampas Woodpecker, a congener of our Flicker. It is more boldly colored and marked than our Flicker, but resembles it in its propensity for "anting" on open ground, and I sometimes found it, always in pairs, far out on the pampas.

I cannot omit mention of one large fowl that appears to be common wherever there are marshy reed-beds in Argentina and Paraguay. This is the big Ypecaha Rail, larger than our King Rail and the most beautiful of all rails known to me in its colors and markings. It is shy enough, but shows itself in the open about the reed borders more than our rails, so that one sees it frequently where it occurs. One that I flushed from reed-beds along the shore of the River Plate precipitated itself into a eucalyptus tree, where it remained in precarious balance on a slanting limb, an unheard-of thing for a rail to do.

I have given here only a small part of my observations in the grasslands of southern South America, listing only some of the birds I saw, and the total of my observations might better be cast in hours than days. What conclusion should one draw from this passing glance, which still revealed to me riches beyond expectation?

Hudson never returned to his native pampas because, I feel sure, he did not wish to impose the spectacle of a depleted nature on his memories of a better day. Unable to accept what he could not prevent, he turned away from it. In his London exile, a solitary man, he turned his eyes inward to a past that survived only within his own memory. I have no such personal memory. To imagine the pampas unfenced, unbounded, I must visit them and, standing on the elevation of Hudson's natal heath, eliminate the existing fences from my mind's eye. I look at the pampas, so flat that automobiles now cross them at random, and easily imagine myself on horseback in a day without fences or automobiles. I am more thankful for what is left than aggrieved at what is gone; for my generation has grown up in an age in which one must take heart at what survives the ignorant iniquity of man and the blight of civilization. Enough of the past is left to give hope for the future. Nature is infinitely persistent and adaptable. But the dictum of Hudson has not lost its application: "the forces of brutality, the Caliban in man, are proving too powerful; the lost species are lost for all time. . . ."

Throughout my visit to Hudson's home that Sunday afternoon, picnickers who had driven out from nearby Quilmes (I doubt that they had ever heard of Hudson) were wantoning with their guns among the little birds that hid from them in the reeds of the Arroyo Conchitas. I eliminate them, too, from my mind's eye, but their work of destruction may be forever.

ON REREADING "GREEN MANSIONS"

FEW books that have gained a place for themselves in English literature are so universally misunderstood and misinterpreted, it seems to me, as W. H. Hudson's *Green Mansions*. The custom is to label it a "fantasy," which is to say that Hudson presented in it an unreal world of his own invention, like that in which Gulliver traveled or Alice's Wonderland. Illustrators, overlooking the explicit statements and precise descriptions in the text, contribute drawings full of fantastically stylized trees, monkeys, snakes, and birds that disport in impressionistic or surrealistic limbos of the imagination. From many readings of the actual words, however, as well as from a familiarity with the American tropics that provide the setting, it seems to me plain that *Green Mansions*, far from being a fantasy, is in fact a nature book, to my mind the supreme achievement of our literature in the description of nature. No one but a great naturalist, a great observer of living nature, could have written it.

In its physical setting *Green Mansions* is a faithful copy of nature throughout: not a tree, not a leaf that is in any way strange to actuality. It begins in a city called Georgetown, which you can find on any map of South America. Georgetown is the capital of British Guiana. The year is 1887. The protagonist is a man called Abel, a political refugee from the neighboring republic of Venezuela. The book is his personal account of his adventures, adventures of the spirit as well as the body, during the years that he wandered in the wilderness of southern Venezuela before reaching Georgetown. In the first half year of his exile he wandered as far as Manapuri, a settlement on the Orinoco River between the mouth of the Meta and the village of San Fernando de Atabapo (look at the map), where he fell ill of a low fever and was forced to stay some months. Throughout this period he kept a journal, and his cherished dream was that he would someday return to Caracas and write a book about his adventures that would win him fame in his country, perhaps even in Europe. This ambition, never deep-rooted, was superseded by another when at last he resumed his travels. The tale of gold to be found in the unknown territory west of the Orinoco filled his imagination, as it had that of others, with the dream of boundless wealth. It led him to a remote settlement of savages at the western extremity of the Parahuari mountains, where the greatest of human adventures was to befall him.

Thus far Abel had been just another educated young man with an adventurous disposition and resourceful character. He was quite undistinguished in his hope of fame, his quest for gold, his unawakened spirit. But here in the Parahuari country, unexpectedly as is always the case, came the revelation, the awakening. One evening after a rainy day he had gone out to sit on a stone and bathe his feet in a cool stream, to be alone with the despair that was his at having found no gold for all the weariness and hardship he had already endured. The rain had stopped, the sun was setting through a rosy mist, flocks of birds (a kind of troupial) were flying overhead on their way to their roosting-place. This passage is short, rare, and not to be defiled by critical comment. The whole theme of the book is anticipated, however, in one statement that occurs here: "I felt purified and had a strange sense and apprehension of a secret innocence and spirituality in nature—a prescience of some bourn, incalculably distant perhaps, to which we are all moving." Gone, from that moment, are the dream of fame and the lust for that yellow metal which had brought him so far. That prescience which touched him so lightly at first was the beginning of a new and final quest.

Up to here, the account of Abel's adventures is like

any straightforward narrative of actual travel, distinguished only by its literary felicity and scrupulous verisimilitude. Troupials, it should be noted, are not birds of fantasy. The descriptions of river and forest, savanna and hill, of birds and insects and persons, are immediately recognizable to anyone who has traveled in the tropical wilderness of America. The account of the Indians, their primitive customs and psychology, is plausible and interesting to the anthropologist. This superbly disciplined realism continues throughout the rest of the book, but now on a higher plane, on the plane of the spirit.

Abel, touched by his vision, remains at Parahuari, where he spends his days wandering in a nearby forest that is avoided by the Indians out of some superstitious fear. As he is drawn more and more to the forest, absenting himself for long intervals from the company of his barbarous hosts, they begin to regard him with an increasing suspicion that soon verges on fear and hostility. Meanwhile, the personal experience, the prescience that had first come to him on the banks of that stream, comes to him again and again in the forest, no longer so distant, in the form of a musical warbling that he distinguishes among the innumerable bird voices, or indirectly through particular adventures, once with a band of Howling Monkeys, again with a coral snake. The account abounds in descriptions of nature that take one's breath away with their sheer realism. The reader who has himself been in the woods, has listened to strange bird-calls and the chorus of howlers, has watched the spiders at their hunting and weaving in the dappled shade, recognizes it all with a heightened perception of meaning.

Take one incident only, from among the others. Abel is living alone, like Thoreau, in a hut he has built for himself in the woods:

One night a moth fluttered in and alighted on my hand as I sat by the fire, causing me to hold my breath as I gazed on it. Its fore wings were pale grey, with shadings dark and light written all over in finest characters with some twilight mystery or legend; but the round under-wings were clear amber-yellow, veined like a leaf with red and purple veins; a thing of such exquisite chaste beauty that the sight of it gave me a sudden shock of pleasure. Very soon it flew up circling about, and finally lighted on the palm-leaf thatch directly over the fire. . . .

Afraid that the heat would drive it from the spot, Abel opened the door so that it might find its way out again into the flowered night. But suddenly . . .

. . . the frail thing loosened its hold to fall without a flutter, straight and swift, into the white blaze beneath. I sprang forward with a shriek, and stood staring into the fire, my whole frame trembling with a sudden terrible emotion.

In the context, the reader understands with fearful poignancy the cause of Abel's emotion. What he has just witnessed is the moment of valediction, beauty succeeded by sudden death, life turned to ashes in a twinkling. That beauty and that fall are the theme of the book.

Abel is like Lancelot, permitted for a moment to see the Grail, unworthy to clasp and hold it. But there are no Galahads in this world, only "a prescience of some bourn, incalculably distant perhaps, to which we are all moving; of a time when the heavenly rain shall have washed us clean from all spot and blemish."

I set out to make the point that *Green Mansions* is one of the great nature books, that it contains in its pages the finest and most realistic nature writing we have. This is true, I believe, if only by the test of veri-similitude. That moth, for example, is not identified by a scientific name, but I feel sure that it represents an existing species and might be identified by lepidop-terists from the description—for all that it is a symbol as well. The snake that sinks its fangs into Abel's ankle is referred to by him as a "coral snake," one of the most poisonous known. That is what Abel thought it was. But check the description, which is precise, in a handbook of snakes and you will find that this is not one of the true coral snakes but is in fact a nonpoisonous species which closely resembles them and is called the "False Coral Snake." That explains why Abel does not suffer the terrible consequences which he expects!

The descriptions of scenes and creatures that fill the book are not fantastic or less realistic because the forms are often not identified by their names. Probably there is no place called Parahuari, but the Parahuari mountains are real. Equally real are individual birds that are described without reference to taxonomy. No nature writing ever possessed more verisimilitude than the following passage, for example:

At one spot, high up where the foliage was scanty, and slender bush ropes and moss depended like broken cordage from a dead limb—just there, bathing itself in that glory-giving light, I noticed a fluttering bird, and stood still to watch its antics. Now it would cling, head downwards, to the slender twigs, wings and tail open; then, righting itself, it would flit from waving line to line, dropping lower and lower; and anon soar upward a distance of twenty feet and alight to recommence the flitting and swaying and dropping toward the earth. It was one of those birds that have a polished plumage, and as it moved this way and that, flirting its feathers, they caught the beams and shone at moments like glass or burnished metal. Suddenly another bird of the same kind dropped down to it as if from the sky, straight and swift as a falling stone; and the first bird sprang up to meet the comer, and after rapidly wheeling round each other for a moment they fled away in company, screaming shrilly through the wood, and were instantly lost to sight, while their jubilant cries came back fainter and fainter at each repetition.

The name of that bird, not given here, is merely a label attached by man. What Hudson gives you is the bird itself at the time of its courtship, in all its beauty, in its specific character as nature made it.

Few novels are more devoid of sentimentality than *Green Mansions*. Its realism, however, moves upward as the narrative advances to higher and higher planes of perception until the gross world of flesh is transcended.

I have purposely not referred, until this point, to the forest-girl Rima, the object of Abel's consuming love, because Rima exists on a plane beyond the reach of ordinary critical questioning. She would be there if never mentioned by name, if never described as a body, implicit in every leaf, in every wild creature, in every bird-note. I am tempted to go so far as to say she would be there if *Green Mansions* had never been written. This is something known to those who have themselves heard in the woods the strange notes that can never be quite explained, or have seen hummingbirds in the forest flash and poise for a moment in a gap of sunlight. When the moth falls into the flames it is Rima falling straight from the leafy tree into the fire set by brute men, Rima being consumed to ashes while the barbarians chant, "Burn, burn, daughter of the Didi!"

Hudson, who never actually saw the American tropics, is dead; yet fantasy or no fantasy, Rima still lives, in his book and in the common experience that the book reflects so perfectly:

A minute shadowy form darted by, appearing like a dim line traced across the deep glossy mora foliage, then on the lighter green foliage further away. She waved her hand in imitation of its swift, curving flight, then dropping it exclaimed, "Gone—oh, little thing!"

"What was it?" I asked, for it might have been a bird, a bird-like moth, or a bee.

THE OWL OF ATHENA

THE Acropolis of Athens, towering over the modern city, is flanked by two lesser hills. The Hill of the Areopagus is the site on which, in ancient times, a council of elders met to manage the affairs of the state (until Pericles abolished it as undemocratic). The Hill of the Pnyx is where the Assembly, comprising all the citizens of Athens, met to manage the affairs of the state in more democratic fashion. Near the summit of the Hill of the Pnyx (where today one sees the remains of a plaza enclosed by retaining walls) Meletus stood before the Assembly and accused Socrates of not believing in the gods in whom the state believed, and of corrupting the young. There Socrates stood, a stocky figure already seventy years old, and delivered his defence.

The Acropolis and its companion hills stand above the sea of modern Athens as the Cyclades stand above the Aegean: three islands of antiquity projecting through the center of a modern city, lifted above its touch. The sides of the Acropolis are precipitous; the Hill of the Areopagus is rocky; but the slopes of the Hill of the Pnyx are gentle, supporting a cover of small pines and cypress.

✧

One may be sure that the Owl of Athena, the patron-goddess, was not the Short-eared Owl (*Asio flammeus*). The authorities say it was the Little Owl (*Athena noctua*), a bird no bigger than a Starling. By contrast with the Little Owl, which is nocturnal, the Short-eared Owl is diurnal and crepuscular. It is not one of those owls that get a reputation for wisdom by making mysterious sounds in the night. It is (the books say) a bird of wild marshes and moors (while the Little Owl is at home in town-buildings, and might nest in a temple). But I, who have often looked for the Short-eared Owl in marshes and on moors, have seen it only twice, both times in the heart of a city. The first time it was hunting locusts in a park of Buenos Aires on a Saturday afternoon. The second was in Athens.

From the Hill of the Areopagus we looked down upon it (John and I), gliding, then beating its long wings, then gliding; sailing and swinging and sweeping in loops, in arabesques, back and forth like a gigantic swallow; out over the traffic-clogged pass between the Acropolis and the Hill of the Pnyx (the cars below never knowing) or along the thinly wooded slopes of the hill itself; moving like music, here and there and back again like a gull following a ship. In the full sunlight, tilting to the rhythm of a music unheard, first this way then that (showing its back, then showing its underparts), it was golden—mottled above, streaked with brown underneath. We passed the binoculars back and forth between us while the great flexible bird swung about here and there below, sometimes rising, sometimes coasting down. . . . Twice in quick succession it dove into the pines of the hillside, disappeared, rose again. (Hunting something?) At last it put down among them for good, the exhibition over.

❖

In the Acropolis Museum is the marble relief of a goddess leaning forward, reaching down with her hand to her uplifted foot, adjusting her sandal. Although her figure is that of a girl in her 'teens, one would not think of calling her a girl any more than one would think of calling the Aphrodite of Melos a girl. Her dignity is that of maturity. Neither, however, is she a woman. A Platonic ideal, lacking the imperfection of flesh-and-blood, she is a goddess by definition. (It is the business of art to represent divinity, and that is what it does in the great ages that know divinity.)

One forgets the marble. The flesh of the upper arm is full and soft—it would yield to the touch. The drapery is transparent, revealing the breasts and the fold that forms across her waist as the goddess stoops. Lifted up by the uplifted knee, or falling from the stooped shoulder, it is silent music, in motion as the goddess herself is in motion. It swings and sweeps like a Short-eared Owl about the Hill of the Pnyx.

This marble turned flesh was quarried from the Pentelikon hills that bound the Attic plain north of Athens. Pentelic marble acquires a warm tint with age, being impregnated with iron. It rusts. (Iron oxide is what makes the Parthenon golden. The gold of *Asio flammeus* has some other origin.)

By definition, this dignity adjusting her sandal is not a girl but a goddess. One would make a like statement about the Parthenon (golden in the sunlight) if the vocabulary allowed. Bigger than any mere building, it has the immensity and the repose of a mountain—but not its imperfection. It is a Platonic ideal, complete in itself: as feminine as a goddess adjusting her sandal, as masculine as Atlas upholding the entablature of the sky.

Ruins attract birds. I am surprised that Pausanius, describing ancient Greece in the second century A.D., failed to comment on this. Were the Black-eared Wheatears not darting about the marbles of the Acropolis in his day? Were they not bobbing, were they not dipping their pied tails, then as now? Were there no Swallows and House Martins coursing over and past? No Short-eared Owls? Why does he say nothing about the Rock Nuthatches that hitch themselves over the fallen stones, peer about, then whistle?

Standing in the open air on the Hill of the Pnyx,
addressing the assembled citizens of Athens, Socrates
told how his impulsive young friend Chaerophon
(whose brother was present and could confirm it)
"went to Delphi and boldly asked the oracle to tell
him whether there was anyone wiser than I was. And
the Pythian priestess replied that there was no one."
Standing in the sunlight on the Hill of the Pnyx, in the
stone-paved clearing above the cypress and the pine,
he continued: "The truth is, men of Athens, that only
God is wise, and by his answer he intends to show that
the wisdom of men is worth little or nothing. He is not
referring literally to Socrates, but is only using my
name to illustrate—as if he should say: The wisest
among you is he who, like Socrates, knows that his
wisdom is nothing."

Socrates and the audience he was addressing had a
grand view from the Hill of the Pnyx. To one side was
the Parthenon, standing golden upon the Acropolis.
To the other were olive groves in the plain below,
stretching to Phaleron Bay, the harbor of Piraeus, and
the island of Salamis. Beyond Phaleron, blue and hazy
in the distance, was the Saronic Gulf of the Aegean,
and the fading coast of Attica running south in loops
and headlands toward Cape Suniun (land's end).

But this was a familiar view and the Athenians,
including Socrates, had other matters on their minds
that day. (Socrates, in any case, never looked outward,
concerning himself only with the inward view.)

All men, however, are not of the same mold. I
picture one young Athenian who, during the long
speeches, allowed his attention to stray. Perhaps a
Short-eared Owl passed in migration, or a company
of Swallows.

✧

The authorities take too parochial a view (judging
other ages by their own) when they report that the bird

of Athena was the Little Owl. It was no more the Little
Owl than the Centaur was a horse. The ancient Greeks
didn't distinguish species as we do. They knew nothing
of the trinomial system of classification based on the
invented taxonomy of Linnaeus (1707-1778). They
knew nothing of *Athena noctua indigena.* The bird of
Athena was not flesh-and-blood at all; not a zoological
specimen but a symbol of wisdom, capable of representation not in flesh-and-blood but in marble (since it is
the business of art to represent what Socrates himself
could not possess, being mortal).

✧

The shrine of Apollo at Delphi is, traditionally, the
abode of eagles. In an eagle's view Delphi nestles
among the feet of Parnassus, that sacred mountain
where eagles, gods, and muses alike are at home.
(Even in mid-April Parnassus is covered with snow.
Presumably gods and eagles are indifferent to heat or
cold, but surely not the muses! Not even Urania, Muse
of Outer Space.)

One authority has identified the "eagles" of Apollo
as Griffon Vultures (*Gyps fulvus*); again, however,
this is the projection of a modern illusion on the past.
As the Aphrodite of Melos has more dignity than a
mere girl, as the Parthenon has more scale than a
mere building, so Apollo's eagles could not have been
Gyps fulvus. They were eagles of the mind. By the
exaltation of divinity they shared what belongs to the
Owl of Athena. (What belongs to the Owl of Athena
is not less real for having been conceived in the mind.
Conception is the beginning of all reality. Think what
it may lead to!)

✧

The marble ruins of the shrine of Delphi lie in a
cleft of mountains that ascend by stages to Parnassus.
Downward from its level an escarpment falls to another

land and climate, to the remote Valley of the Pleistos
winding below toward the Gulf of Corinth. (The Gulf
of Corinth, distantly seen from Delphi, is the same
hazy blue as the Saronic Gulf distantly seen from the
Hill of the Pnyx.) The gray-green of the valley-floor
represents olives of endless age, an unbroken grove
extending to the white port of Itea (just visible) where
the ferry leaves every morning for the Peloponnesus.

Still today the soaring birds of Parnassus patrol the
precincts of Apollo, as in the day when young Chaerophon came so boldly out of Athens to ask whether
anyone was wiser than Socrates—and got an answer
that posed a problem for Socrates only.

The air lifts along the face of the escarpment as the
morning sun heats the land below. Then the great
birds rise up on it like steam. Perched at the brink,
one sees them approaching out of the depths, circling
up. First it is a Lammergeyer, immense of wing and
tail. In an instant it has swept past, showing the black
tufts under its chin, the baleful white eye looking out
through its black eye-patch. Then it is soaring above,
leaning over and drifting toward Parnassus. Another
Lammergeyer follows. Then, one after another, birds
of other species, parading from below, exalting themselves above us, regarding us not (although it was we
who had once accorded them divinity). The Lammer-

geyers are followed by two Griffon Vultures (their naked necks projecting through white fur collars),

then by two Egyptian Vultures and a Golden Eagle. They spiral up through the rabble of Ravens that swarm about the rocks and cliffs, rising above and beyond. . . . (Sometimes the Ravens rise with them.)

These are not the eagles of the gods. What brought them down from Parnassus in the morning light was— not any spell of the Pythian priestess but garbage. There is an ecological chain here. The tourists, coming to view the ruins, are housed in the tourist hotels at the top of the scarp: a by-product of their housing is the garbage dumped over the edge: the great birds descend daily to breakfast on it before rising again to the heights.

The need to feed on garbage represents the difference between us mortals and the immortal gods conceived by us.

Looking at these Platonic ruins, we easily forget that the ancient Greeks shared the penalty of mortality. The Delphic Oracle attracted a profitable business not altogether unlike that which the Delphic ruins attract today, and the birds must have shared in it then as now. There was death and garbage in ancient Greece too.

❖

Zeus (who almost gave swans a bad name when he fathered Helen of Troy) has his shrine at Olympia in the Peloponnesus, the site of the Olympic Games. The local boys now play soccer in the stadium where naked athletes once competed for the laurel crown (the Crested Larks rising above them, spilling their song over the field, then as now).

Those who assembled here for sport and worship, like those who assembled on the Hill of the Pnyx, were not distracted by birds. But John and I are. Guide-book in hand, moving about the tumbled remains of the Bouleuterion (the administration building for the Olympic festivals), we are distracted by a repeated series of clicking calls from an adjacent grove of low pines.

Abandoning scholarship at last (like boys playing hookey), we creep into the grove toward the sound. . . . Sudden silence. Then, as suddenly, two large birds (just perceived through the branches) shoot from a tree, swerve among the trunks, and vanish deeper in the grove. A moment later—again the clicking from a new station. Owls, I think, having been awakened last night by two Tawny Owls in conversation by the window, having owls on my mind still. (But it wasn't owls.)

Twice more we flush and lose the swift birds. Like arrows released from a bow (behind the pines), they shoot off too fast to be made out. Or like boomerangs, for they swerve back (in and out among the trunks) to another part of the grove. (The grove, if the flyers are to remain within it, is too small for straight flight at such speed.) Then one of them, swerving across a beam of sunlight, comes out as in a stroboscopic flash, every feather left clear in one's momentary memory— the golden-brown back, the gray-barred underparts, and the long banded tail of the adult Goshawk.

Now back to study with the guide book. Where is the Bouleuterion? (But who would have thought of Goshawks?)

❖

The Goshawk is not a classical but a mediaeval bird,

associated with spruce forests and gothic lands, with darkness. What is he doing in this shrine of Zeus—unless Zeus, in this one world of ours, is also Wotan?

❖

I supposed, being misled by the Platonism of the books, that it was always summer and sunshine in ancient Greece. That was why girls and goddesses could wear the weightless drapes that neither hid nor hampered their bodies. That was why the athletes could enter the contests naked. It had not occurred to me, until visiting Greece in early spring, that the audience gathered in the theater at the foot of the Acropolis to see the new drama by Euripides might have been washed out by the rain; that the orator addressing the Assembly on the Hill of the Pnyx might have had his words flattened against his mouth by the north wind, while the unhappy citizens in attendance clung to the flapping corners of their chitons; or that it might have been necessary to postpone the Olympic Games on account of weather. On the morning of April 2, 1963, a naked discus-thrower in the stadium at Olympia would have been performing in the rain.

❖

When Agamemnon ruled in Mycenae (and was betrayed by Clytemnestra) society was still so primitive that it was proper for King Odysseus of Ithaca to build his own house with his own hands, and himself guide the plow behind his oxen in the spring plowing. (On the seagirt island of Mykonos, watching a farmer plow his field with a heifer and mule yoked together, we remembered how, on another seagirt island, Odysseus, pretending to be mad, yoked together an ox and an ass to plow his fields.) Civilization, following upon the invention of agriculture, was just beginning in that age; the successor to the Neanderthal and Crô-

Magnon men was just emerging. Just emerging, and going someplace—but we cannot yet tell where.

The next six or eight centuries, to the Age of Pericles (and a goddess adjusting her sandal), showed a remarkable advance, and there has been a remarkable advance since (although the goddesses have dropped out, the owls have lost their wisdom, and the eagles have become vultures). A world of difference separates King Paul in his residence at Athens from King Agamemnon in his residence at Mycenae (three hours' drive, three thousand years away).

There has been no like change, I think, among the birds.

The citadels of the Achaeans and of their successors were built on high places looking out over a coastal plain to the sea, but not on the coast itself, for fear of pirates. At Mycenae the citadel of Agamemnon has a backing of mountains from which it overlooks the plain of Argolis to the Gulf of Argolis (hazy blue, like the Saronic Gulf seen from Athens, like the Gulf of Corinth from Delphi), and beyond to the dim mountains of Arcadia, capped with snow. The land that was once fertile has now been sterile—for how long I don't know. A few generations of Agamemnon's predecessors (using goats) might have reduced it to the rocky barrens that the avifauna of barren places inhabits today. If so, Cretzchmar's Buntings (their round eyes as innocent in their baby-blue heads then as now) must have sat about as unsuspiciously on the Cyclopean stones *tseeping* and *tsipping* then as now—although Homer, in his description of Mycenae, remains strangely silent about them. In the shrub-hollies that grow in the ravine toward the Persia Spring there must have been Sardinian Warblers, birds that Clytemnestra may have admired (but not Electra, who was a serious girl). Also Subalpine Warblers with red throats. The Hooded Crows flapped back and forth—over the plain, over the citadel. The Lesser Kestrels (blue on head and

tail like the blue of the Gulf of Argolis, golden on back)
darted and turned about the towers of Mycenae in
companies, like swifts, attracted by human community
then as now.

✧

Every year, for the celebration of Apollo's birthday,
Athens sent a sacred ship (the one in which Theseus
returned from the conquest of the Minotaur) to the
sacred island of Delos, his birthplace. Until it returned
no public execution might take place, with the consequence that a month had to pass after Socrates had
been sentenced before he could be served the hemlock.

Then, one day at dawn, Crito came to Socrates in
his prison, saying: "Socrates, I bring bad news—not so
bad from your point of view, I suppose, but bad for us
who are your friends. . . ."

"What?" said Socrates. "Has the ship come from
Delos, on the arrival of which I am to die?"

"No," Crito replied, "it hasn't actually arrived, but
it will probably get in today, according to some people
who have just come from Cape Suniun, where they
saw it. Therefore tomorrow, Socrates, will be the last
day of your life."

The S.S. *Despina* left the port of Athens (i.e., the
Piraeus) on the 5th of April to take us to the sacred
island of Delos, where we would pay our respects to
the memory of Apollo—now dead. (He was dying while
Socrates was alive, and it was in a pitiful effort to save
him that Socrates was killed.)

Rounding Cape Suniun, stopping at Andros and
Tinos, she got us into port some thirteen hours later.
(The life of Socrates would have been shortened if she,
instead of the ship of Theseus, had been the sacred
vessel.)

Cape Suniun, the point of Attica, is thirty miles
from Athens. If we suppose that, coming overland, it
took Crito's informants two days to go the distance, or

one day if on horseback, then it must have taken the ship of Theseus two or three days, just from Suniun.

The Temple of Poseidon, gleaming white in the sunlight on the high headland of Suniun, represents divinity to mariners who see it from afar, today as twenty-three hundred years ago. Like the Parthenon on the Acropolis, it is a beacon.

The sea, though dark, is "wine-dark" only where wine is blue. It is dark enamel-blue, streaked everywhere with the white of the high wave-crests, for the north wind (Boreus) streams over its surface all day long, day after day. The Manx Shearwaters, in their hundreds off the Attic coast, can cope with it. They ply their sharp wings in the trough of the wave, never rising above it, following its changing contours. The Herring Gulls follow the steamer, making the wind serve them.

Between Kea and Andros—a fluttering speck in the trough, a land-bird struggling against the giant wind, keeping low like a shearwater, making small progress with great exertion. A lofty Herring Gull, itself at ease, slides off on one wing and dives at the struggling speck, which rises up high on the wind in the hope of escape. (Now one can recognize it, by its zebra stripes, as a Hoopoe.) The gull, however, loses interest and allows itself to fall away down the wind. The Hoopoe descends once more to the trough, resuming the Odyssey of its migration between continents.

No ship goes direct from Athens to Delos any more. Delos is the most insignificant of the Cyclades, a rocky projection with hardly a tree on it or a shrub (and with no harbor for a modern ship). It is just off the much larger and more imposing island of Mykonos (where one goes to visit it)—and, on its other side, the much larger island of Rhenee. Yet it played a nobler role in the history of ancient Greece than any of the other islands.

For the visitor, looking at this seagirt speck and contemplating its fame, the question arises: Why Delos? Why Delos among all the islands that amount to something?

The answer is that here Apollo was born.

But this merely begs the question. What humor was it that caused the God of the Sun to be born on Delos?

The answer to this is a lesson to mankind. Leto, having become pregnant by Zeus, was turned away from one Greek community after another, each fearing the vengeance of the great god's lawful spouse, Hera. Driven from city to city, from island to island, she ended by coming to the most insignificant spot in the Hellenic world, and there at last she found asylum. The greatness of little Delos stems from the unique charity of some poor shepherds (or fishermen) who inhabited it. After that, no spot in Greece was more sacred.

Delos first comes to the world's notice as the refuge of a delinquent girl who bore in her womb Apollo.

❖

The tub of a boat from Mykonos plunges through the sea—plunges and plunges again, with a shower of spray at the bottom of each plunge. Forever climbing up the climbing wave, forever plunging into the trough of the wine-dark sea, sending up its shower of spray. . . . Boats like this have been plunging through these waters ever since the heroes of old sailed for Troy, ever since one of them took ten years to return.

There is no real harbor on the sacred island (except one attainable in calm weather only). Instead, the boat comes up in a hatful of calm water behind a rock, to which one leaps from the gunwales. (The returning hero would have appointed half his men to explore

inland—to find Circe or Cyclops, Calypso, the Cattle of
the Sun, or who-knows-what?) It is overland, now, to
ruins out of all proportion to the island in their scale
and fallen magnificence.

They say the Lion and the Lizard keep

The Courts where Jamshyd gloried and drank deep

There are not two marble stones together without a
lizard poking its nose from the crack between them,
or slipping over their surface. Beside the common
green lizard there is, here, a dragon seen nowhere
else. It is black with a yellow, armor-plated head—
bigger, slower, and less fearful than less fearsome
lizards. (I also saw an adder among the ruins, showing
that the sea was later in separating these islands from
the mainland than in separating Ireland, or that they
had no St. Patrick of their own.)

The Lion also keeps these courts, and I don't know
how to account for his universal presence. He is in
stone—over the Lion's Gate at Mycenae, along the
Avenue of Lions at Delos, tumbled from the eaves of
the original Temple of Athena on the Athenian Acropolis, rending bulls on the fallen pediment of the same
temple. I suppose the ancient Greeks knew the great-
maned Lion of Barbary from their visits to North
Africa—or perhaps it still occurred, as once it had, on
the European shores of the Mediterranean. Perhaps
in the days of Agamemnon there were lions in the
hills behind Mycenae.

✧

Parian marble, as white as alabaster, must be the
most attractive to birds and lizards (as to sculptors).
I know no other way to account for the life concen-

trated among the ruins of Delos. One can walk all day over the rest of Delos, or over Mykonos, and find Crested Larks not uncommon. But among the Parian ruins of Delos they are as abundant as lizards. On every block of marble, on every column standing or fallen, they perch and sing. They chase each other in and out through the courts, calling and singing on the wing. And White Wagtails. And two Black-headed Wagtails, never before seen by the visitors (guide-book and binoculars in hand). And Ravens and Hooded Crows, Swallows and swifts (big Alpine Swifts and little black Swifts), coming and going overhead. . . .

At the lowest part of the ancient site, by an inlet of the sea, the marble floors of the courts are temporarily carpeted with sheets of water or of mud. Here are Little Ringed Plovers and Wood Sandpipers, rising on rapid wings before the visitors, piping as they go. (The guide-book has nothing about them.) These birds, too, are the beneficiaries of the charity of the shepherds of Delos.

Clumps of spear-grass have grown up at the edge of the ruins, making a sort of marsh. It cannot be an acre in extent and, for all I know, is the biggest marsh in all the Cyclades. Yet I saw a crake (Little Crake or Baillon's Crake?) disappear among the grass-stalks as we passed. Who would have expected a rail in a ruin?

❖

Ravens, which in the rest of Europe (as in North America) are now found only in high mountain-wilds or cliffs bordering the sea, were once the scavengers of towns and cities everywhere. W. H. Hudson reported that they made themselves at home in London through the first quarter of the nineteenth century. Only in Greece have I seen them still enjoying this ancient association. In the central Peloponessus they feed on garbage and carrion in the outskirts of the towns. In Nauplion and in Mykonos they course over the house-tops (in Delos over the ruins).

❖

Notes for a new guide-book on Mykonos: At the end of the road that runs south from the town (across the isthmus that connects the main island with the *presqu'île* beyond), at a white chapel on the blue sea, there are Swallows, Red-rumped Swallows, and House Martins; Wheatears and Black-eared Wheatears; in early April, Meadow Pipits. On April 7, 1963, a bird landed in a gray sandy field on the isthmus, looking (perched) like a sand-grouse from the Gobi Desert. Then it lifted up into the north wind on flicking wings —now looking like a small tern of exotic color and markings, the underside of its wings raven-black (with chestnut hinges), its forked tail black and white. It was a Pratincole—sacred, surely, but to what divinity has not yet been established.

❖

On April 9 the woodless island of Mykonos was visited by Wood Warblers on migration. (Wood Warblers out of the woods are as fish out of water.) One found refuge in the exotic ornamental shrubbery of a hotel-garden. Two others were together working their way northward across the barren highlands of Mykonos, clinging to overhanging rock-faces and flitting about the crevices of stone walls like Wall Creepers. At night they would (like the Hoopoe) brave the north wind to fly on over the ocean, in the wash of the waves (looking for woods)—to Tinos, to Andros, at last to Euboea and the mainland. There, and in the mountains of Thessaly and Thrace, they would again find the shelter of massed trees.

On April 10 the grove of pine and cypress on the slopes of the Hill of the Pnyx (once visited by a Short-eared Owl already arrived, presumably, in central Europe) is full of Wood Warblers (on their way after the owl—as we are too, at last).

✧

Travel is dangerous for birds and men. (Odysseus had shared the danger of the Hoopoe in the trough of the wave.) When I leave Geneva to go to Greece, when I leave my home in the twentieth century to visit Hellas, I hold my breath until the weeks of wandering are over, until home-life is restored, the family reunited. The Wood Warblers, even on Mykonos, can have no greater sense of the precariousness of this our life than I have. I am one with Odysseus and the Hoopoe.

In his seventy years Socrates never left Athens except on military service, and once when he went to Corinth for a festival. He was the most constant home-stayer in a city of travelers. This, clearly, was not because of insecurity. He simply wasn't interested in the external world, the world of sights and sounds. He wouldn't have noticed a Short-eared Owl if it had perched on his head (though he knew the Owl of Athena well). He considered the external world worthless.

(The authorities differ over whether Socrates actually held the theory that ideas are primary, the material world secondary, or whether Plato's attribution of it to him was simply a literary device. I submit, in evidence, his abstinence from travel.)

In the *Phaedo* he asks whether sight and hearing have any truth in them, concluding that they have precious little. "Is not thought best," he asks, "when the mind is gathered into itself, when it becomes as free as possible of all bodily sense?" The *idea* of beauty was what counted for Socrates, not any representation of it. He told Cebes how, in his youth, "I was afraid that my soul might be blinded altogether if I looked at things with my eyes or tried to apprehend them by the help of the senses."

Socrates was no kind of observer at all. At the beginning of the *Republic* he is persuaded by Polemarchus to remain in the Piraeus for a public festival lasting all night, including a torch-race on horseback in honor of Athena. "We will go out after dinner," says Polemarchus, "and look on."

But they don't. Instead, they remain in Polemarchus's house talking, the festival forgotten.

This is typical of urban intellectuals. I met a New York friend upon his arrival in Geneva for his first visit to Europe. It was one of those lovely days when Geneva, set at the end of its lake like a jewel, is momentarily touched with a forgotten divinity. Driving him from the airport to where we suddenly came out on the lakeshore and the glory, I said: "There, before you, you see the Lake of Geneva!"

"Now take John Foster Dulles," he said. . . .

"Over there," I went on, "with the sunlight on it— that's Mont-Blanc."

"Or look at what Adenauer's doing in Germany," he continued. . . .

(I spend my life in conversations like this.)

Can anyone doubt what would have been the nature of the conversation if I had met Socrates at the airport?

Kant in all his eighty years never left the vicinity of his native city, Königsberg, where he preoccupied himself with pure reason.

("Now take the categorical imperative. . . .")

✧

Observation, I think, is more exhausting than thought. It wears a man out sooner. Philosophers live the longest.

The observer goes through this world as through a museum crowded with masterpieces, room after room. He is enlarged by the wonders spread before him, and humbly grateful. After years and years and rooms and rooms, however, at last he begins to feel the accumulating burden of so much wealth. He begins to foresee a time, however distant yet, when the prospect of taking his departure will no longer be unwelcome (when the Owl of Athena, grown heavy, has almost ceased from flying). He will at last look forward to his arrival at an airport that he had been trying, all through the long dream of his life, to remember—the airport that will turn out to be. . . .

✧

It is three hours by air from Athens to Geneva, three hours to return from the past to the present. How long is it, then, from the present to the waiting future? Perhaps a reader who someday unearths these lines will know.

O, rest, brother mariners, we will not wander more.

EPILOGUE: THE RELIGION OF SEDGE

Sedge is a land that no outsider except me has ever visited and reported on fully. Pluvis, who is mentioned in the following extract from my report, was one of the leaders of the Sedgian society and my mentor during the three years of my sojourn in Sedge.

I HAVE been puzzled to know how I might approach the subject of religion in Sedge. The reader may grasp the difficulty when I note that Sedgian thought and language is incapable of making a clear distinction between religion and art. I take a chance of misleading when I use our English terms, but since I cannot escape their use I may say, with precaution, that in Sedge the artist, the musician, or the literary craftsman is, if not a priest, the nearest thing to one. (There are no priests in Sedge.)

Sedgian art, in the first instance, is the description of nature. This, says the artist, is what mountains are like when a drifting mist half obscures them. This is a bird hovering in the spray of a waterfall. This is a boy pulling a fish from the river. This is a spruce tree in a sudden gust, shaking off its burden of snow. This is an old man with a melon. This is a girl-child asleep.

The Sedgian artist does not, however, say: This is one particular scene, or this is a particular person. He may draw his mother, taking care with the likeness, but what he is describing is woman when she has lived long enough to achieve completion. One might say that what he is describing is completion.

The artist depicts the visible in order to reveal the invisible within it. He paints flesh to catch a meaning that is not flesh. In the woman he sees completion, and in completion itself something deeper. One cannot be precise about these matters and I shall not labor to express what can only be experienced. What the artist depicts when he describes nature, when he describes the bird hovering in the spray of the waterfall, is revelation. He sees the bird as St. Paul once saw a vision on the road to Damascus.

I could write a technical discourse here on Sedgian music, proving rightly or wrongly that it too is the description of nature, that it describes movement apart from what moves: the quick running step of the fox, but without the fox; the repeated dip, tug, and release of the willow tips in the running stream, without willows or stream; the drift of a cockle boat on the rippled surface of a pond, without boat or pond. But this would be to describe the abstract concretely. The very act of description falsifies.

Sedgian music delights especially in separate movements traveling together, the harmony among them. Each is an individual life of its own, not just an accompaniment to others; but all these, whole in themselves, together make a grander whole, and behind this grander whole, again, something more is revealed.

The Sedgians do not make the distinction we do between sacred and profane art, sacred and secular music. Pluvis could never understand it, and when I tried to explain it to him I became uncertain myself. I explained that if an artist paints a picture of the Mother of God to hang in a church he is practicing sacred art, while if he paints a picture of his own mother to hang in his home he is practicing profane art. But one can make no sense of this in the Sedgian language because it amounts to saying that this art is art while that art is not art. When I explained that Johann Sebastian Bach wrote sacred cantatas for performance at church services and secular cantatas for wedding feasts he asked me what significance such a distinction could have. I answered that the purpose in the one case was to support the worship of God while that was not the purpose in the other case. But if you begin by defining art as religion, then such a distinction is meaningless and it was meaningless to Pluvis.

What I am trying to do here is to introduce the subject of Sedgian religion. It has its expression in the graphic arts and music. But one looks for something more definite and formal as well, a doctrine, a theology. So one turns to Sedgian literature.

Literature is the most versatile of the arts, since it can describe physical nature only less vividly than drawing and can convey abstract movement only less purely than music. Sedgian literature has its share of descriptive writing and poetry that, like art and music, reveal meaning in nature. But literature has, further, the unique distinction of being able to express meaning explicitly and logically. To the sensitive observer the picture reveals meaning as by a secret communication, but only in words can one sometimes say what the meaning is—even though the words inevitably falsify it. I shall try, therefore, to summarize Sedgian religion to the extent that it is made explicit in the philosophical literature of Sedge.

The Sedgian sees the cosmos always in two aspects, which I may as well call "the perfect" and "the imperfect." In virtually every respect he inhabits these two worlds: in his appreciation of nature, in his statecraft, in his family life, in the conduct of his own career. This duality is, to him, the prime fact of life, and it is so impressed on him from his earliest consciousness that he would hardly be capable of seeing otherwise than with this double vision. The acceptance of this view is so complete that it is simply assumed in Sedgian literature. Although one finds no explicit expression of it, one finds no explicit account of the world that is not based upon it.

What is visible in the artist's drawing is the imperfect world; what is invisible is the perfect world. A musical composition, because it abstracts from what is tangible, is a more direct expression of the perfect world, though not necessarily more vivid.

The reader may have observed to himself, by now, that this dual view represents, simply, Plato's theory of ideas. This may be true, but in the Sedgian mind the duality has a comprehensiveness, a pervasiveness, and also a sort of indefinability that quite distinguish it from Platonism or any Greek thought. Plato would have said, of the tangible bird hovering before the waterfall, that it was an imperfect representation of the idea of bird. To the Sedgian the bird is part of an omnipresent perfect universe that is damaged at the last minute by the process of being translated into what is tangible. It is also damaged in the process of its apprehension by our senses. It is like a straight pencil-line on paper, which is really one-dimensional, though a close examination would show that in the imperfection of its rendering it had breadth as well as length. Again, one might say that the line is perfect in its straightness, even though a close examination showed that the artist's hand trembled. The imperfection has as little significance for the reality as the distortion caused by a mirror.

In this dual view, the gravitation of all life is inescapably in the direction of the perfect world. This direction is compelling and not to be questioned. It represents something like divine intention. The trembling of the artist's hand does not make the line less straight in reality, but the artist must strive, nevertheless, to keep it from trembling, to reduce the gap between the imperfection and the perfection. The bird in the spray of the waterfall strives toward the realization of its own perfection, since it is governed by the same compulsions as men are, and the artist strives in the same direction when he draws it. Although reality is perfect, the flaw always occurs at its birth— the flaw in the bird, the flaw in the picture. It is against this that all nature is directed. The bird is flawed, but the artist's rendering less flawed, representing a closer approach to reality than the original itself. The rhythm of a bird in flight is not as close to its own reality as that rhythm translated into music. I am speaking metaphorically here, trusting the reader himself to apprehend the meaning behind the metaphor. When I use the word perfection, that is not literally all I mean.

The artist or musician is striving to realize, more than the reality of the bird, the reality of a perfect universe, and the bird itself is ultimately inconsequential.

All life is a process of creation, following the model presented to us by what I have crudely called revelation. The question arises how the process got started, whether it represents a guiding will. The answer that a Pluvis gives is that he cannot possibly know. Less sophisticated Sedgians refer to "God," conceiving him, I gather, in whatever terms fit their individual minds. Simple persons, the majority, think of him as a Sedgian worthy and even know the place of his abode. Those who are somewhat less simple may have a more abstract notion of him, entertaining in their minds a deism to which they attach no image. And though persons like Pluvis, representing the greatest sophistication, are humble agnostics, God is still a part of their vocabulary and logic—though the term may for them be synonymous with "the unknown." They see the manifestation and assume something behind it, but disclaim any ability actually to see through to its origin.

The simple enjoy a pleasant traditional legend of the Creation. God has from the beginning been frustrated by a mischievous devil bent on marring his handiwork. God created the universe and while it was still wet the devil threw a handful of sand against it. The devil causes landslides, smudges the scenery with his thumb, pours mud into the water, plucks the tailfeathers from birds, causes the fox to miss his footing, and gets innocent women with child. The tales of his pranks are endless, and I gathered that the Sedgians are rather fond of him.

At a more serious level the devil wears a more malevolent aspect. He corrupts the hearts of women who would otherwise be faithful to their husbands; strikes blind the seeing; poisons the wellsprings of the human spirit; stands between man and God's revelation; interferes with grace.

On the most sophisticated plane he is entirely abstract, but nonetheless real. Pluvis, for example, believes that there are two principles in the universe: the creative principle and a principle, not precisely of evil, but of something like sabotage. In a sense, this is merely a description of the universe in terms of its duality, which he cannot doubt.

What is implicit in these conceptions is a view of the universe and life as essentially good but subject to a frustrating or tormenting element, the element that will always succeed to some extent in defacing the good, will always make the artist's hand tremble. What is also implicit is man's mission and his duty. Man is good but, like all things, has within him the element of destruction. Against that element, which prevents the completion of the universe, he must contend. Pluvis is no less sure of this than the simplest peasant in Sedge.

In this ambivalence between good and evil man is not distinguished from the rest of nature. He is not more drawn toward perfection than is the fox or even the rock on the mountain. This is a conception distinct from the Christian belief that only men have souls, that the capacity for divine perfection is theirs alone.

In practice it is evident that the most important element in life is something like what we would call divine grace. Man, of himself alone, is capable of achieving nothing. He cannot, perhaps, even get the hay in and safely stored, or build a house, or keep his footing on the edge of the precipice, except with grace.

The Sedgian would understand that line of the psalm which reads: "Except God buildeth the house, they labor in vain that build it." All men, therefore, live by grace in some measure, but especially the artists, the literary craftsmen, and the musicians. That vision of the invisible which they set down in their compositions is a manifestation of grace conferred on them individually. They are in a state of grace when they work, for they could not work otherwise. Grace not only allows the artist to see the invisible but, to the extent that his hand does not tremble, this is what does it. There is here something of the Greek conception of the muses, the artist's sense that his creation represents, not his own self-expression but divinity expressing itself through him. By God's grace he has been chosen as the essentially passive medium.

All this has its points of vagueness and even its contradictions, but it is thus that it appears to exist in the diverse manifestations of the individual Sedgian consciousness. We are, ourselves, so used to associating the idea of grace with the idea of original sin that I find some contradiction in a view of man as essentially good and still so dependent on grace. The essential goodness of man, in the Sedgian view, may be a manifestation of the abundance of God's grace. But there is no use trying to shape these concepts into a more logical and consistent system than they represent in Sedgian thinking itself.

The important thing in practice is that everyone feels his dependence on grace, the agnostic no less than the believer in a personal god. This is controlling, for it impels everyone so to conduct himself as, he believes, will make him worthy of grace. In a simple peasant this may call for ritual; in a Pluvis it calls for a humble heart, a commitment to truth, and faithful dealings with others. And I suspect, although this is in the realm of his privacy, that Pluvis, the agnostic, prays.

I need hardly say that the dual view of the world and man's mission in it gives rise to the hope of a day when God's perfection will no longer be marred.

Alexander, W. B., *Birds of the Ocean*, New York-London, 1928

Austin, Oliver L., Jr., *Birds of the World*, New York, 1961

Beebe, C. W., *The Arcturus Adventure*, New York, 1926

Blum, Harold F., *Time's Arrow and Evolution*, Princeton, 1968

Bourne, Bill, "Gulls and London's Airports," *British Trust for Ornithology News*, February 1969

Chapman, Frank M., *Handbook of Birds of Eastern North America*, New York, 1932

Darwin, Charles, *The Various Contrivances by which Orchids are Fertilised by Insects*, London, 1882

———, *The Voyage of the Beagle*, New York, 1915

Fisher, James, *The Fulmar*, London, 1952

Frank, Philipp, *Einstein: His Life and Times*, New York, 1965

Géroudet, Paul, *Water Birds with Webbed Feet*, London, 1965

Goudge, T. A., *The Ascent of Life*, London, 1961

Gray, Asa, *Gray's New Manual of Botany* (revised by Robinson and Fernald), 7th edition, New York, 1908

Griscom, Ludlow, *Distribution of Bird-life in Guatemala*, Bulletin 64, American Museum of Natural History, New York, 1932

Halle, Louis J., *Men and Nations*, Princeton, 1962

Hardy, Alister, *The Living Stream*, London, 1965

Hudson, W. H., *Birds of La Plata* (2 vols.), London, 1920

———, *British Birds*, London, 1895

———, *Far Away and Long Ago*, New York, 1918

———, *A Hind in Richmond Park*, New York, 1923

Lerner, I. M., *The Genetical Basis of Selection*, New York, 1958

Medawar, P. B., *The Future of Man*, London, 1960

Murphy, Robert Cushman, *Oceanic Birds of South America* (2 vols.), New York, 1936

Murton, R. K., and Clarke, S. P., "Breeding biology of Rock Doves," *British Birds*, Vol. 61, No. 10, October 1968

Peterson, Roger Tory, *A Field Guide to Western Birds*, Boston, 1941

Peterson, R. T., Mountfort, G., and Hollom, P. A. D., *A Field Guide to the Birds of Britain and Europe*, London, 1966

Scott, R. F., *Scott's Last Expedition: The Personal Journals*, London, 1923

Summers-Smith, D., *The House Sparrow*, London, 1963

Venables, L. S. V. and U. M., *Birds and Mammals of Shetland*, Edinburgh, 1955

Voous, K. H., *Atlas of European Birds*, London, 1960

Wetmore, Alexander, *Observations on the Birds of Argentina, Paraguay, Uruguay, and Chile*, Bulletin 133, U. S. National Museum, Washington, D. C., 1926

Whyte, Lancelot Law, *Internal Factors in Evolution*, London, 1965

Witherby, H. F. (ed.), *The Handbook of British Birds* (5 vols.), London, 1943/44

THE species mentioned in this volume are here listed alphabetically according to the vernacular names used in the text. Each such name is followed by the scientific name, which gives genus as well as species, and then by any alternative vernacular names widely used in English or, for South American species, in Spanish. Where a vernacular name represents British as opposed to American usage this is shown by adding "(Br.)" after it; where it represents American usage as opposed to British "(Am.)" is added.